# EASY
## parenting

# EASY
## parenting

# Ken & Elizabeth Mellor

FINCH PUBLISHING
SYDNEY

Busy Parents Series

**Easy Parenting**

This edition first published in 2001 in Australia and New Zealand by Finch Publishing Pty Limited, ABN 49 057 285 248, P O Box 120, Lane Cove, NSW 1595, Australia.

The material in this book was first published as part of *ParentCraft: Essential skills for raising children from infancy to adulthood* by Ken and Elizabeth Mellor (Finch, Sydney, 1999).

03 02 01   7 6 5 4 3 2 1

National Library of Australia
Cataloguing-in-Publication entry

Mellor, Ken.
Easy parenting.

Bibliography.
Includes index.
ISBN 1 876451 11 4

1. Parenting.  2. Child rearing.  3. Parent and child.  I.
Mellor, Elizabeth, 1938–.  II. Title.
(Series: Busy parents series).

649.1

Text designed and typeset by 𝒟𝒾𝒽𝑔𝓃
Edited by Shelley Kenigsberg
Illustrations by Andrew Bell
Editorial assistance from Ella Martin
Cover design by 𝒟𝒾𝒽𝑔𝓃
Cover illustration by Andrew Bell
Index by Emma Barber
Printed by McPherson's Printing Group

# Contents

# Introduction

This book is designed for busy parents. The pressures of life today are so great that many of us have little time for extras. We need ready access to information and to ways of doing things that quickly make a difference in our lives. Rarely do we have the time for extensive research into the many options that are available today. The content and style of this book have been chosen to fulfil these needs as completely as possible.

We parents want our children to thrive and grow into healthy, happy adults. As busy parents, we also need to receive suggestions that are easy to understand, work well, and are flexible enough to adapt to many different situations. To do what is required of us, it also helps to have some level of confidence in the guidance we receive from others. We want to get it right with our children. Every chapter in this book is brimming with suggestions that hundreds of parents have used successfully with their children. They have stood the test of time.

## Finding advice or help

A detailed table of contents and an extensive index give you two easy-to-use ways of finding what you need. As well as this, every chapter has headings and subheadings arranged obviously so you can discover the contents quickly. You will usually be able to find what you are looking for after only a little reading. To cater further for the needs of busy parents, the material is presented in succinct, manageable bits so that you can dip into it for a few minutes at a time, for example, just before going to bed. This is not a book that requires long reading sessions.

## Adapt what you read

We hope that what you find here will help you to raise your child or children as easily and as well as possible. Many parents have told us how clearly written it is, how much they now know that they did not realise before, and how practical and helpful they found the suggestions. We are naturally delighted with this feedback. All the same, your family, your children and your home situation are unique, so you will certainly need to adapt our suggestions to make sure that what you are doing truly suits your own and your children's needs. Taking several attempts as you learn how to use some of the approaches is completely normal.

## Our sources

Our original sources for the book were other parents. Over the years we collected as much information as possible from people who were raising or had raised their children successfully. We needed this help in our efforts to take care of the hundreds of children with whom we were involved directly or indirectly over the last 30 years.

The most immediate source of this material is *ParentCraft: Essential skills for raising children from infancy to adulthood* (Finch, Sydney, 1999). While some of the material has been modified, most of it remains unchanged. The only significant addition is that some 'parent messages' are repeated with children in different situations.

## Our experience

Over a period of 30 years we have worked with children in various ways, including  as social workers, psychotherapists, parent educators, family counsellors, and staff members in custodial and other institutions for children and young people. For all this, our most important qualification is that our own daughter is now in her early twenties, so we have experienced all the processes first-hand.

# Chapter 1

# Parenting with love

Some people find it natural and easy to love, while others do not. And very commonly, most people find that their love ebbs and flows in the face of their children's behaviour and their own preoccupations.

In this chapter, we take a look at love, four ways to express it, and how to practise each if we are not good at it. This is the most important chapter in the book.

# Let's talk about love

Love is fundamental to everything we do as parents. It is the ground in which our children grow and the sun that shines on them as they do. Well-loved children thrive; love-starved children wither. This relationship is obvious to most caring people. Nevertheless, many people have not understood this, even in the recent past. Fortunately, we are living in more enlightened times than many others have.

Love draws people together and promotes growth. It nurtures, warms, soothes, teaches, heals, integrates, enhances, honours and respects. Love dissolves boundaries and separations between people. It draws people together in appreciation of each other. Very importantly, it makes our young capable of loving and being loved. It promotes sharing, mutual knowing, understanding, celebration of each other and complete union. This is really powerful stuff!

Unfortunately, many children are not loved as they need. Sometimes this is to do with the parents, sometimes to do with the children, sometimes both. Whatever the cause, the absence, or filtering of love is a great loss. It creates wounds and unmet needs, deprivation, and a sense of rejection or violation. It makes rifts between people. Unloved children usually grow into adults whose capacity to love themselves or others is stunted or distorted. Fortunately, we can do a lot to change all of this if we need to. More on this later.

## Messages for children

'I love you.'
'You're terrific.'
'What a great person you are.'
'I'm glad you're my son/daughter.'
'I'm proud of you.'
'I'm so glad I'm your mother/father.'
'You're special/beautiful/wonderful.'
'I love everything about you.'

# The secret to 'making' love

Love is the most needed experience in the world. Of all experiences, it has a unique impact on us. It is perhaps, also, the most wanted and the most sought after. So wonderful when we share it, we usually want more and more. Apparently so out of reach when we don't have it, we can spend our lives in search of it.

The secret is simple. Every experience of love we have involves joining with another in some way. With the joining, we drop our separateness from one another and allow aspects of ourselves to blend. The more complete the oneness or union we have, the more intense the love is.

> Love and union always go together.

- You lie with your baby on your chest, just experiencing the moment, and feeling expanded by the intensity of the love you feel with your child.
- You sit cuddling your child, staying aware of each other as you do.
- Your child says, 'I love you, Mum', or 'I love you, Dad', and you feel your heart melt.

It is very much up to each of us. When we concentrate on what brings us together with others, what we like about them and love about them, what we enjoy, what we agree with, and what we share, we promote love. You can do this with anyone, although in this context we are discussing parents and children.

- 'I love the curl of the hair on your neck.'
- 'I really like the fun we have together.'
- 'You are so trusting and open with me. I love you doing that.'
- 'I delight in the way you tell me what is important to you.'
- 'Your laugh, your sense of humour, your ..., delight me.'
- 'I love *you*.'

By contrast, we only need to do the opposite, if we want to reduce love. To do this, we create separation. We probably all do it at times. With these thoughts or statements, love often dissolves.

- 'You don't tell me you love me.'
- 'I feel let down by you.'
- 'You should do what I tell you and you aren't.'
- 'You didn't do ... and I don't like it.'
- 'Whenever I express my love to you, you do something distracting, like talking about something else, or finding something to do that takes you away.'

'Making' love is simple. When you want love, then join with people. If you don't want it, then create and maintain separation.

# What love is not

Love is love. Love is beautiful, obvious, varied and wonderful. However, some people confuse themselves about love; they quest for what it isn't. Love is not:

- the *desire for love*
- the feeling of *not wanting loneliness*
- the *yearning or emptiness we feel* when we do not feel love
- the *hope that we now have it*
- the *pretence* that we have it
- the *loss we feel* when it goes
- the *distress* at not having it

# Four loves

Our children need us to love them in four different ways. Each makes a key contribution to the way they grow up and the sorts of people they become. They are:

- 'Body love'
- 'Feeling love'
- 'Person love'
- 'Being love'

Combined, these four ways of loving release powerful forces into everyone's life.

# 'Body love'

Children need lots of physical contact every day. Most delight in touching, looking, listening, holding, caressing, smelling, and kissing. They love having physical nurturing from us. It is very clear that a special physical pleasure is shared with affectionate touch.

To experience this love, arrange time so you have physical contact with your children, and notice the pleasure while you do. Feel the loving union produced by the sharing.

- Lie or sit in a warm bath cuddling your baby.
- Hold your children close when they lean against you.
- Take their hands and hold them for a while as you read a goodnight story.
- Have long hugs frequently.
- Sit on the couch cuddling up together.
- Look warmly at your children as they look at you.
- Sound warm, loving and nurturing as you talk to them.
- When they are excited, exclaim with them as you grab them into a quick, exultant embrace.

> 'Body love' comes from sharing physical pleasure.

By contrast, touch disturbs some children. They may squirm, wriggle, resist, tense up or cry when touched. These children still need touch, and our job is to help them learn to accept it.

## Practising 'body love'

If you or your child is uncomfortable with touch, we recommend that you practise until you are both used to it. You can put yourself or your child on a simple daily program.

Do physically loving, caring and affectionate things with your child and with others. Start with small steps. You could start with smiles, or a touch on the arm; saying something simple like 'Hello' or 'Hi there' makes it easier at times, too. Then gradually expand to longer contact, then to brief hugs, then to longer ones. Persist with the expansion, for years if necessary.

## 'Feeling love'

We nurture the emotional lives of our children by expressing 'feeling love'. For their sakes, we need to envelope them in this feeling. As often as possible we express our love to them, feeling it as we do. Sometimes strong, sometimes subtle, this love is very distinctive.

The feeling of love is centred in the heart. It flows from the heart into the rest of the body, saturating it with warm melting sensations. The body softens in response to this energy, a sense of mellowness develops in the sounds we hear and a soft fuzziness grows around the edges of what we see. Everything tastes sweeter and more fragrant to us. Acting impulsively as we feel it, we would reach out and gather our children into a loving embrace.

> 'Feeling love' comes from sharing feelings and emotions.

When we love our children like this, they melt into us. Our love automatically conveys understanding, acceptance, openness and sharing, just with the feeling and nothing else. It leads to a wonderful openness that enables children to open up to us and to share their feelings about things. And, interestingly, it is the sharing of any feelings – even uncomfortable or challenging feelings – that stimulates this love.

All you need to do is make opportunities for emotional sharing. Open yourself emotionally to your children. Find out what they feel and share your feelings with them.

- Tell your children how much you love and enjoy them.
- Encourage your children to tell you that they love you.
- Talk to them about their feelings and accept what they tell you.
- Encourage them to tell you their feelings about you.

Do this during everything from a chat at the kitchen sink to a 'deep and meaningful' anywhere.

All feelings change from moment to moment – and love is no exception. Completely well-balanced people experience a whole range of feelings, only one of which is love. Other feelings like anger, happiness, sadness, security, and fear are all completely normal. So relax if you find yourself not feeling loving towards your children at times. It is normal for us not to feel loving towards them, for example, when they are acting up, or we are tired, or we or they are simply distracted by other things. This does not mean that we do not love our children. We always have two other forms of more enduring love that we can call on – 'person love' and 'being love'.

## Practising 'feeling love'

If you need a bit of practice, we have some suggestions. We express 'feeling love' very much in what we say and how we say it. So using 'hearty words' as often as possible is wonderful. A short list is: 'caring', 'affection', 'tenderness', 'cherish', 'lovely', 'warm', 'love', 'friendly', 'admire', 'adore', 'considerate' and 'devoted'. Say, 'I love you' to your partner and your children often. If the word 'love' is too strong in the beginning, use other words such as 'care for', 'like', or 'enjoy'.

To make the way you talk loving, practise noticing your physical heart as you talk. Also, drop your voice into your chest, rather than speaking from the throat or the head. The extra depth and resonance from there has a very different effect from the more watery sound of the throat, or the higher pitch of the head. Learn to soften your face and smile a little as you talk.

Make yourself available to love and affection from others. When others 'reach out' to you, reach back, so you join with the people who are trying to join with you. You can do this physically by returning someone's touch. Or you can do it in other ways. When people acknowledge you, notice it. If they compliment you, accept the compliment and absorb the warmth behind it. Saying, 'Thank you' can be a good first step, as it interrupts the tendency of some people to push away gestures of affection with a quick comment or distancing act. Remember that love accompanies union.

# 'Person love'

We nurture the individuality and wholeness of our children by expressing 'person love'. It is the loving delight we have in 'the people our children are in themselves'. By loving them as whole people throughout their childhoods, we encourage them to find, express and value their own individuality.

'Person love' goes with acceptance, appreciation and understanding of our children as separate people. They are not here for us, they are here to fulfil their own lives. If you have ever known this kind of love, you will know what we mean.

> 'Person love' comes from appreciating someone as a whole person and sharing that with them.

'Person love' has a constancy about it. Not bound to daily events in the same way as 'feeling love', it extends beyond the moment. To do with understanding and thought and perception, it is neither physical nor emotional, like the first two. It is, nevertheless, quite distinctive.

To encourage 'person love', take opportunities to open up and share who you are with your children. Notice who they are and encourage them to reveal that to you. Also, get them to notice it themselves. Our children develop the capacity to do this surprisingly early.

- Ask your children what is important to them.
- As they grow up, find out what kind of person they want to be.
- Tell them what you, as a person, value in your life.
- Find out their opinions on things before giving your own.
- Show respect for their points of view, values and integrity.

Some parents see their children's 'personhood' clearly at all times and love it automatically and easily. Some only see it in glimpses, when a curtain seems to pull back and reveal the whole person inside the baby, the three-year-old, the adolescent. Whenever we do, our love affirms, 'Wow. That's you, is it? Well, great to meet you. I'm here for *you*. I'll do whatever it takes for you to grow up and *fulfil* who you are'.

This love prompts us to celebrate their expanding maturity. Every new milestone is a cause for joy, not for regret. Powerful and enduring, 'person love' is a force that we parents can use to endure through the years of childhood. It helps us to get up night after night to our children, to go to work for years to support them, and to forego our own pleasures repeatedly to ensure their wellbeing. It also helps us to do all the tough things that raising children involves.

## Practising 'person love'

To love like this well, the first thing to do is to stand back from your children and take a distant look. You need to understand them from outside your own routine responses to them. Get out of the habit of them, and into their reality.

- Think about the children next door. Describe them briefly: 'nice boy', 'intelligent', 'happy', 'mature'. Then, using the same general stance, do the same with each of your children.
- Imagine you have just met your family. What sort of people are your children?
- Imagine what others would notice about your children.
- Get some friends to describe your children to you.

The next step is to accept your child as a person and celebrate who he or she is. We can say things to them like, 'I love who you are', 'You're great', 'I am here for you', 'Do what you need to do in your life', and 'You are important to me'.

Each day, hold each of your children in your awareness, then imagine them growing like beautiful plants. Appreciate that, while you nurture and tend the plants, the final beauty is already in them. Celebrate this, unite with it and love them.

## 'Being love'

There is much more to all of us than our bodies, feelings and personalities. Through 'being love' we embrace everything in our children. With this love, we open up to and embrace their destinies, their individual meanings and their purposes. In this love, we experience complete acceptance of our selves and the selves in them.

> 'Being love' comes from sharing our beings.

Transcendent, eternal and all-encompassing, this love is in everyone and everything. It comes with 'the touch of divinity' in us all. And as we join with our children through it, 'we touch their divinity with our own'. Doing this floods all our lives with transcendent grace at every level. We share a contact that is so profound, we aptly call it 'soul-to-soul contact'. And this contact transmits our 'soul appreciation' of them, to them.

We experience 'being love' either as we come into union with our own beings, or as we join with the beings of others. This process is very specific and not mysterious in the least, for those who have experienced it. We have a joyous, peaceful sense of oneness with everyone, including our children, when we experience this love. To experience it:

- Practise noticing the core of your children.
- Notice how the person in front of you is an outlet for, or surrounded by, something bigger.
- Regularly engage in some form of spiritual practice.
- Share your spiritual perceptions, understandings and experiences with your children.

Increasing numbers of people now knowingly love their children like this. They are fully aware of what they are doing. We think that this is a lot to do with the spread in recent decades of personal spiritual practices throughout the world. Even so, as with the other three types of love, many people have not been aware of experiencing this kind. So our description may not mean much to you at the moment.

If you are not aware of having experienced this kind of love, you may get some clues from reasonably common events in your life. We do go through times in our lives when 'being love' is very available. It is very strong in situations in which the life force is very powerful, or when it is powerfully challenged:

- at the birth of a baby;
- when we are in love;
- when someone is very ill and approaching death;
- during near death experiences;
- at the point someone physically dies; or
- when we are with evolved people such as spiritual masters.

## Practising 'being love'

To become familiar with this love, we can cultivate total acceptance of ourselves and others. A very simple exercise or meditation helps us do this.

Sit comfortably and notice your heart for a few minutes. Put your hands over your heart and notice any warmth, mellowness, soft light or sweetness in there. While doing this, repeat, 'I am love'. Keep doing this for a short time. Then, allowing anything about yourself to occur to you, say 'I love you; I completely accept you'. This could be anything specific from the shape of your nose to much more general things.

After doing this for as long as you want, take each of your children in turn. Do the same thing with them. Start again with, 'I am love'. Then move to repeating, 'I love you (name); I completely accept everything about you'. After a short time, allow their various qualities to occur to you, affirming as they do, 'I love your (quality) and completely accept you'.

Spending two to five minutes a day doing this, increasingly produces a wonderful, loving connection with your own essence and the essences of your children.

Also, look for and seek opportunities to link 'being to being' with others. Find people who seem good at it and imitate them.

# Combining the four

The four loves are always mixed in together. Enjoying the sensations of love, feeling the feeling itself, appreciating the understanding we have of the people involved, and celebrating their beings, all go together delightfully. Everyone we know does experience all of these, whether they know it or not, at least to some extent. We have never met anyone who has managed to suppress these four kinds of love completely. However, we have met many people who are better at some of the four than others.

The thing to realise is that our children need all four from us, if they are to thrive fully. So it is well worth practising those we are not good at, until we are. Both our children and ourselves will benefit.

# But what if I don't feel love?

People don't automatically feel love for their children. Perhaps the children were premature, or the mother or child was sick and normal bonding did not occur at birth. Perhaps the children are not our physical children: maybe they are step-children, or adopted, or the result of artificial insemination by donor. Or maybe they are very difficult to live with. Some children are, for example, extremely needy, or competitive, argumentative, passive, or passionate in ways that we find difficult. And even if others would take such things in their stride, we don't. What then?

You have company. And with persistence, you can develop connections and flowing ease with your children. We suggest that you give yourself time, talk about your feelings and reactions to someone you trust, and persist in doing what your children need. Remember that 'being love' and 'person love' are powerful forces and may not be accompanied by much feeling. If you are troubled significantly by what you are or are not feeling and thinking, seek help from people who are competent to provide it.

# Chapter 2

# The discipline sequence

Discipline helps our children learn to manage their energies. All people need to learn this so they can live easily and well with others. In this chapter we discuss what discipline is, when to start disciplining our children, how to start, and the discipline sequence. This sequence is a simple way of handling specific disciplinary encounters.

# Discipline is guided love

Discipline is an organised way of expressing love. We said in the last chapter that love is like the ground in which a plant grows and the sun that shines on them as they do. Discipline is what the gardener does to fertilise, water, prune, shape, stake and generally respond to a plant's growth to ensure it reaches maturity as beautifully as it can. Guiding what we do with our love, we act to produce desirable changes in our children's behaviour, when they need this from us.

Discipline is our means of 'house-training the kids'. Everyone benefits from this. Without training, they will rarely learn to live well in the world. They often become unruly, unreliable, discourteous, self-absorbed, messy, uncaring, impulse-driven people – or worse. At the same time, the advantages of discipline include more than other people's convenience and comfort. Discipline is for the benefit of our children too. Well-disciplined people can command themselves and take the many opportunities life offers them.

> From discipline, children learn the power of making decisions and the freedom of acting on them.

## Messages for children

'Thinking you can do something is the first step.
Feeling you can do it in the second step.
Actually doing it is the last.'
'Make decisions about how to act and follow through on them.'

# Two parts to discipline

We generally do two things with discipline. We *set standards* and we *set limits*. The two things support each other in important ways.

*Standards* involve what children are to do. They are what children aim for, what we encourage them to achieve. If we list our standards, we have a set of rules, prescriptions, advice and guidelines that would enable our children to live life well.

- Brush your teeth after every meal.
- Tell the truth.
- Share with others.
- Do what you say you will do.

*Limits* involve what our children are not to do. They are supposed to avoid doing these things and we actively discourage them from doing them. If we remove the word 'don't' from a list of limits, we would have all the things to do to get into trouble in life.

- Don't act violently.
- Don't leave your room in a mess.
- Don't talk rudely.
- Don't be late.

## Combining the two

When disciplining children, we find it works best if we set standards and limits together. One gives the things to do; the other gives the things not to do. When we do this, our children know more clearly where they stand. The result is a much more confident child. A friend once described this very well:

> 'When I grew up, I was mainly told not to do this and that. I don't ever remember being told what to do, except in very general terms like "be nice" and "do the right thing". And I wasn't ever told what these meant. So I got to adulthood and I was really uptight. I mainly knew what not to do, but I felt that

*I never knew when I was doing the right thing. It was like living in a box with lots of spikes pointing towards me and I didn't know where all the spikes were.'*

We have found the following guideline very helpful when deciding how to combine the setting of standards and limits. **You set standards that automatically take care of the limits you are also setting.**

- 'You're to tell the truth to me (standard); you're not to lie (limit).'
- 'You're to touch your sister gently (standard); you're not to hit or hurt her (limit).'
- 'You're to listen to me when I talk to you (standard); you're not to keep watching TV (limit).

> To stop our children doing something, get them to do something else that makes the first thing impossible.

## Messages for children

'What you put out, you get back. So always think carefully about what you do.'

'When doing things you don't like, figure out how to make them as enjoyable as possible.'

'Do with others what you want them to do with you.'

'Listen to what I say, and do what I tell you immediately.'

# The age to start

The age to start disciplining children is at about eighteen months. Near that age, they begin to develop new levels of understanding and ability. They also start to do things that prompt us to shift gears and to start to expect them to adapt to the world. They will no longer be the centre of life. Gradually, they need to learn that everything does not come to them whenever they want it, that the world does not revolve around them. This is quite a contrast from what we have done up to this point. Before eighteen months, children still have baby consciousness and they need to be cared for as babies. (You will find more on the transition in Chapter 3, 'Standing to decide' and Chapter 8, 'Developing self-esteem'. Also, look at *ParentCraft*, Chapter 20, 'Four births, four bonds' and Chapter 21, 'Phases of childhood'.)

Babyhood is a time for our complete, continual and loving acceptance of our children – no matter what. This is definitely the time for 'being love' to be at the forefront of everything we do. (See Chapter 1, 'Parenting with love'.)

Babies are innocent, totally dependent, alive, questing, exploring, loving, trusting, vulnerable little creatures. Babies don't have self-control, nor have they developed any significant understanding. They depend totally on us for everything. It is our job to provide for them to the best of our abilities, without applying any discipline to them.

We wish to state this very clearly. *It is completely inappropriate to discipline babies.* They are incapable of controlling themselves and of understanding consequences related to what they do. Disciplining babies in any way is an abusive violation. We realise many people don't understand this. Parents all too often:

- punish their babies by shouting at, hitting, or shaking them;
- withdraw attention when they think their babies aren't good;
- think their babies are misbehaving;

- talk about crying as nastiness or an attempt to punish parents;
- think it is wrong for their babies to do something just for attention;
- describe their babies as naughty.

If you do any of these things, or anything similar, we urge you to stop for your child's sake. Learn to love your babies with complete acceptance. Whatever they do, continue accepting them and, with nurturing love, take care of whatever needs to be done.

If you cannot manage this, then get some help. Disciplining babies does untold damage, damage that can last for life. It tilts or distorts the foundations inside them, so that what they build on for the rest of their lives is tilted or distorted too. We have worked for many years with the consequences of this kind of thing, which is why we are presenting this to you so strongly.

> Always love, nurture, care for and protect your baby. Never discipline your baby.

## Commands for everyday living

| | |
|---|---|
| Stop. | Stand still. |
| Come here. | Move quickly. |
| Move away. | Talk to me now. |
| Go away. | Keep still. |
| Hands off. | Hold my hand. |
| Drop that. | No. |
| Let go. | Pay attention. |
| Keep safe. | Stay away. |

# Introducing discipline

One of the wonderful things about young children is that they are so obvious. And the signal they give us that they are ready for discipline, is very obvious.

At about eighteen months they begin to struggle with those around them. They may switch into this quite suddenly, although more usually, they gradually increase the intensity and frequency. Distraction and soothing stop working to calm upsets. Our children become determined to get what they want and hold out for much longer than previously. They act angrily and persist in their little miseries, rather than allow themselves to be coaxed out of them. At the same time, parents often begin to feel increasingly impatient, where before they were likely to feel calm and inclined to soothe and console.

Whatever change we observe in our children at this time, we introduce children to discipline *gradually*. A sudden shift from complete acceptance to conditional responses is likely to create unnecessary upsets. However, we do need to make the shift and this can take determination. After all, we have had almost two years of finding out what our babies want and need, so we can soothingly supply it. At this stage, however, while we remain interested in what they want and need, we become increasingly inclined to expect them to adapt to us. This is a shift of gears for both our children and ourselves.

We begin by acting with increasing insistence over what we want our children to do. And even if they become upset as we do this, we persist.

- 'No. You have to wait for your milk. I'll get it in a minute.'
- 'It's time to eat. Come and help me clean up your toys now.'
- 'You are going to bed now, so calm down and do it easily.'
- 'No, mummy (daddy) can't play with you just now. But you can play here beside me.'
- 'You can have milk or juice, not ice cream. Which one will you have?'

Parents not used to persisting through their children's upsets can become very upset at this stage. For some parents, this can feel like reason enough to give up the whole idea very quickly. The loving strength to persist is inside us, however. We find it in 'person love', the love that gets us to think of the person we are raising, not just the baby who doesn't want her milk right now. (See Chapter 1, 'Parenting with love'.)

Persistence is far better than 'falling into the coaxing trap' of continuing to treat our children as babies. This is where we avoid confrontations by trying to find ways of soothing and coaxing our children to do things they don't want to do.

*One family was caught like this with their first daughter. Because she made a fuss, they stopped telling her insistently to go to bed. Instead, her father used to 'entertain her' up the stairs. He would move backwards out of the living room, doing all sorts of things to try and engage her so that she would follow him. By the time she was three years old, he was having to dress in a full clown outfit to get her to bed. If he was a clown when she was three, what would he have to do by the time she was fifteen?! It would have been far simpler to train her differently from the beginning. We would have recommended saying, 'It's bed time', then setting off immediately hand in hand, or with her in his arms, so going to bed became an easy routine.*

### Messages for children
'You are to do what I tell you.'
'You sometimes have to wait.'
'Do it now, so you can go and play.'
'You can choose — milk or juice.'
'Look at me when I talk to you.'

# How to use discipline

We use what we call 'the discipline sequence'. Its five simple steps guide us through what we need to do so our children get what they need from us.

The steps of the sequence are:

1. **Expectations**   Say what you expect of them *and* what you limit them from.
2. **Reasons**   Outline why you are saying this.
3. **Consequences**   Set consequences for compliance and noncompliance.
4. **Agreements**   Get agreement(s) about the future.
5. **Follow-up**   Ensure that you get what you expect.

Here is an example.

(Expectations) *'I expect you to come home at 10.30 pm. You are not to return later.*

(Reasons) *You are still too young to decide how late to be and we have to make sure you are safe.*

(Consequences) *If you keep returning at 10.30, we will quickly be convinced of your reliability and more likely to be relaxed about you getting home later. If you don't, then we will not allow you to go out.*

(Agreement) *Do you agree to come home at 10.30 pm?'* Then, of course, your child agrees immediately!

## Messages for children

'You can think and feel at the same time.'
'Things don't just happen, you do them.'
'You can change what you do, by deciding to.'
'Ask questions when you don't understand.'

# Expectations

Expectations need to be clear to everyone involved. This means that they need to be understood and preferably unambiguous, otherwise confusion and avoidable difficulties can arise. Making them specific often takes care of all of this.

- 'If I can hear the TV through the door, it's too loud', rather than 'Keep that noise down to a reasonable level'.
- 'Keep your hands to yourself, or touch gently (showing young children what gentle touch is)', rather than 'Be gentle (nice, or loving)'.
- 'Come to dinner at 6.00 every night', rather than 'Be on time for dinner'.

Remember to set both your expectations and your limits. Telling children both what is expected and what is not acceptable is important. It is surprising what adults and children miss at times.

> Expectations make clear what is to be done and not done.

*An adolescent boy called Alfredo was on the point of expulsion from high school. He was acting very violently every day.*

*The teachers 'had tried everything for months, but to no avail'. When a consultant asked exactly what teachers had said to Alfredo, everything became clear to her. The list included, 'Get out, you know you're not supposed to do that', 'Go and see the principal', and 'We'll just ignore Alfredo, won't we, class? We don't like what he is doing'. Because they all thought it was obvious, no-one had told him explicitly what they were disciplining him for. But Alfredo actually had no idea what he was doing to get into trouble.*

*A program was devised for him. From then on, every incident of violence, was followed by a clear statement about what he had done that was not acceptable, and what he was to do in future that was acceptable. For example, 'If you are frustrated, don't hit people or throw the desks around. Sit quietly, put your hand up, and I will come across to you and talk to you as soon as I can'. Within three weeks, he was behaving completely normally.*

# Reasons

Children have their own reasons for doing things, just as we do. Finding out what their reasons are is important. For example

- 'I wanted to, so I did.'
- 'You told me to put everything in the bin; you didn't say not to put the plates in too.'
- 'I kicked him because I thought he was going to hit me. I didn't know he was going to pat my head.'

Whatever **we** think their reasons are, we need to connect with **their** reasons. What we do to change their behaviour will have much more impact, if we explain it so that they understand. Just the act of asking why they did what they did, also helps us to keep them engaged in the process.

Our reasons are important too. By telling them why we do what we do with them, we train them in all sorts of important ways. We teach them to think about themselves, so they take account of other people and situations. They can also learn that just because they have reasons, doesn't make them right.

Discussing reasons gets children to think about their actions.

We recommend that you talk so that your reasons are easily understood. Match them to the understanding of your children. (Notice the increasing sophistication of the examples.)

- 'Ouch, that hurts. Stop it.'
- 'Other kids don't want to play with kids who hit them.'
- 'Hitting hurts and people don't like it.'
- 'Acting kindly attracts people, acting nastily will probably drive them away.'
- 'If you want to be a caring person, you will take care of others. Hitting and screaming abuse at them is not consistent with this.'

# Consequences

We use consequences to add weight to what we tell our children. We choose the consequences to encourage them to do what we want them to do and to discourage them from doing what we don't want. We have found several principles useful when we think about consequences. The first one is the main one.

*Reward children for successfully meeting expectations, in preference to penalising them for nonperformance.* What we concentrate on we get. So we are best to emphasise meeting our standards by rewarding our children for doing so. Our incentives can include anything from specific physical affection and verbal praise, to material rewards, to expansions of privileges, to special events or celebrations.

All the same, the reality is that children also need active discouragement at times, if they are to learn. We use the following principles to help formulate what discouragements to use.

*Relate consequences to the interests and desires of the child.* For example, being sent to his room might be just what Tom wants, because he loves spending time alone reading. So, if this were to be a reward, it would work well, but as a deterrent, it would not be so good. However, he places a lot of value on his weekly pocket money. Losing some of this makes him sit up and pay attention to his father.

*Use minimum force to produce the effects we want.* In other words, avoid using a baseball bat, when a feather will do. Missing out on tonight's episode of a favourite TV program may make the point with enough impact, where losing all TV privileges for a week might not make the point any better.

*The younger children are, the more immediate consequences need to be.* Very young children have no sense of time. So setting a consequence that will last for a week for a two-year-old is futile and oppressive. Whereas a consequence lasting for a week might be just what an eleven-year-old or a sixteen-year-old needs. Also, young children need consequences applied very much more quickly than older children. Young children might not even remember what they have done, if we wait too long.

*Act respectfully while resolving problems or issues.* Children get more from ending a disciplinary encounter with our respect. Resolution is the goal, not holding things against them. They need the chance to move forward free from the current incident. So leaving the issue behind is very important, once they have settled things well enough. Also, during the process of resolution, we need to remain open to the possibilities of change, even when we are sorely tested to commit to the opposite. So avoid statements such as, 'You'll never amount to anything', 'I'll never trust you again', or 'You never do what I tell you'.

*All consequences (aimed at limiting) are selected to shift discomfort, so the*

Consequences encourage children to act as expected.

*child is motivated to act as expected.* Our consequences need to 'bite'. The whole idea of consequences related to limits is that children both notice them and dislike them. When they bear little relationship to the acts, issues, or events involved that prompted us to act, it is best to clarify the connections.

*Ensure that uncomfortable consequences stop as soon as the child changes the behaviour.* 'Punishment for its own sake' rarely works. Children generally learn much more by getting relief as soon as they change what they are doing. So as soon as they change, we change.

*Natural consequences make the whole process more educational.* Natural consequences align with the way people in the wider world usually do things. They help to teach our children about the way the wider world works. So a child regularly late for school, may go to school dressed in pyjamas if he or she is not dressed when the car is due to leave; an adolescent asking for a note to excuse him from not finishing an assignment (due to watching TV) gets the option of no note or one telling the truth; or a child regularly not completing her household chores does not get paid her pocket money, because 'she did not turn up at work'.

## Agreements

This step is very powerful. Getting clear agreements usually produces great rewards. It transforms good intentions into actual behaviour. The key ingredient in this transformation is *a decision to act*. And we get our children to decide to do what we want, by getting them to make definite, clearly stated agreements with us.

Without the decision to act, all the good intentions in the world made while the children are under pressure may not amount to anything. They can dissolve at any time.

- 'I *feel like* doing the dishes before going to bed.'
- 'I *want to* get my school assignment done tonight.'
- 'I *really must* get to my paper round on time.'
- 'I *ought to* go and see my teacher this morning.'
- 'I *must go* to sleep now, or I will be tired all day tomorrow.'

The reason these kinds of motivation often don't lead to action is that they are based on feelings. And the moment the feelings change, so does the intention. We may feel very strongly that we want to, should, need to, or feel like exercise tomorrow. But five minutes later, or when we wake up the next morning, we discover that we no longer want to, feel we should, or need to do what we were thinking.

> Agreements turn good intentions into decisions to act as expected.

A decision to act makes a great difference. Commitments endure through changes in our feelings. They 'draw a line in the sand' that shows us clearly what we are and are not going to do.

- 'I **will do** the dishes before going to bed.'
- 'I **will get** my school assignment done tonight.'
- 'I **will get** to my paper round on time.'
- 'I **will go** and see my teacher this morning.'
- 'I **am going** to sleep now.'

So, make sure that you get an agreement from your children about future behaviour. And make sure they put it into their own words, unless they are still too young to do it. The sophistication of the agreement will vary with age.

- 'Will you come to Mummy when she tells you from now on?'
  'Yes.'
  'Good. Now you say it.'
  'I come, Mummy.'
- 'So what will you do about school notices from now on?'
  'I'll put them in my school bag when I get them and give them to you when I get home.'
- 'How will you act with your brother/sister from now on?'
  'I'll talk to him/her about what I want, instead of fighting. And if I can't work it out I'll come and get you.'
- 'Now that you understand the safety issues involved in this, what will you do in future?'
  'I'll come home by taxi when it's after 8 o'clock and I'll ring you whenever I'm going to be home later than I told you.'

## Messages for children

'Keep your agreements.'

'Let others know what you think and feel.'

'If something happens to stop you keeping an agreement, let everyone know as soon as you can.'

'You have responsibilities. Meet them.'

'You can agree now. It's simple. *Just do it.*'

## Follow-up

Follow-up is very important. We need to make sure our children do what we expect them to do. Children rarely learn things the first time, or even the second. They need the repetition. (See Chapter 7, 'Repeating ourselves'.) By following up, we ensure that they have understood and are acting as we agreed they would act. We also need to follow up to apply the rewards or penalties we arranged.

Following up shows that we mean business, too. Our children will take this in and be able to act similarly in their own lives. Follow-up helps us to avoid training our children that discipline is an empty ritual – a lot of words with no real impact. Many children learn 'to wait out their parents', knowing that 'the ordeal' will be over in a few minutes, hours, or days. Because their parents don't follow up, they learn that nothing really matters, because they never get held to account for what they do afterwards. This is not a good idea.

> Following up shows that parents are determined and care.

> Following up teaches children to persist, to keep their commitments and to succeed.

## Struggle is useful

Children learn all sorts of things by struggling with us:
- handling conflict;
- managing their own strong feelings while relating appropriately to others;
- recognising their strengths and weaknesses;
- honing their personal capacities to stand assertively, while staying open to others;
- absorbing from us the strength they need to manage their inner struggles;
- taking in our values and expectations strongly enough to use in their lives.

# Chapter 3

# Standing to decide

'Standing to decide' is a powerful tool for helping our children learn many important lessons. We can also use it to assist us when we discipline them. Children can learn how to claim their power creatively, rather than confusing this with resistance. Parents learn how to influence their children in effective, nonpunitive ways, and without using hitting or other forms of violence. Very simple to use, it helps us to produce wonderful results on many fronts. In this chapter we describe and discuss the process.

# The steps

'Standing to decide' has five basic steps.
1. Instruction
2. Warning
3. Standing with a task
4. Decision
5. Resolution

## Step 1: Instruction

The process starts when your children do something that you want them to change. You say, 'Do X. Don't do Y'. And you give your reasons. This is the instruction.

- If they obey immediately, you reinforce this in some way by acknowledging it. You might, for example, say, 'Good'.
- If they don't comply, you go to Step 2.

## Step 2: Warning

When your children continue to act as before, or do not obey you, issue a warning. You say, for example, 'Do X; don't do Y, or you will 'stand to decide' until you decide that you will do it'.

- If your children comply then, you go no further. You might reinforce the obedience by saying something like, 'You are to do what I tell you the first time I tell you'. By following 'the discipline sequence', you then get your children to agree to act as required in future. To do this, you ask, 'What will you do from now on?' And when all goes swimmingly, they say, 'I'll do what you tell me straight away in future', or words like that.
- If your children still do not comply, you go to Step 3.

## Step 3: Standing with a task

Immediately your children still do not comply at Step 2, you apply the consequence. You point to where the child is to stand and say, 'Go over there, face the wall and 'stand to decide', until you decide to do X'. For example, 'Until you:

- decide to stop stirring up your sister/brother;
- decide to remember to bring your drink bottle home from school;
- decide to go and make your bed immediately;
- make a plan about how you are going to do your assignment;
- have remembered what you decided to do last time;
- decide to stop talking to me rudely and talk respectfully and civilly'.

And you add, 'Let me know when you have decided'.

Your children then 'stand to decide' until they do as instructed. It is most important that they *are able* to do the task you set them at this point. Then you wait, usually with your child in sight.

## Step 4: Decision

You wait for your children to say, 'All right, I have decided'. You then say, 'Okay. Turn around and talk to me about it'. If they seem to take a long time before saying this, or are still learning the process, check every now and then to make sure that they are doing what is necessary.

Emotional upsets during this step are common, particularly when the issues are highly charged. So you may need to stand near them or occupy yourself nearby. Your presence gives you the opportunity to repeat many parent messages about self-management and whatever else is relevant. Think about what your children need to do and put that into words, so it becomes a program they can take in from you.

- 'Calm down and think. Work out what you are there to work out.'
- 'No. You can't have a drink until you have finished.'
- 'You *can* work it out and you are going to stand there until you do.'
- 'I want you to be somewhere else having fun. I don't want you there. So get on with it and do what you have to do quickly.'

# Step 5: Resolution

Check what your children have decided. Make sure they mean to do what they say. Get a specific agreement about how, when and where they will do it. In other words, follow 'the discipline sequence'.

- If all of this flows easily and you have a sense of completion, then release them from the process. You say, 'Okay. Come away from there. And make sure you do what you have said you will'. Follow up and ensure that they do act according to their agreements with you.

- If you are not satisfied with what your children say, then they continue to stand. You say, 'Turn around again until you decide to do X'. If you are not satisfied with the way they are acting, you say, 'Turn around again; stop doing such and such, and do so and so. I am not willing to talk to you while you are doing that'. For example: 'Stop whingeing and whining, and talk in a normal, strong, clear voice', 'Stop shouting at me and talk calmly', or 'Speak strongly and firmly, so I can hear you easily'.

- If you release them and they do not immediately do what was agreed, you go immediately back to Step 2. And you keep repeating the whole process until the child does what is expected.

> 'Standing to decide' replaces hitting and other violence in discipline.

Children whose parents have used 'standing to decide' or something similar are remarkably different from many other children. They are powerful, self-contained, sensitive, clear thinking, assertive, receptive and capable little and big people. They are living testaments to the value of having some way of helping children grow and develop internally.

# How it can work

Sarah, a five-year-old, is engrossed in the TV, watching a late-afternoon children's program. Her mother, Jo, calls out, 'Sarah, turn off the TV and come here. It's time to set the table'. Sarah's evening job is to set the table for the family. *(Step 1 – Instruction)*

No response from Sarah.

Just to make sure she had heard, Jo says, 'Sarah, did you hear me?' If she hadn't, then Jo would repeat the instruction.

Sarah mumbles, 'Yes,' with a rising pitch that signals impatience.

Jo says clearly and firmly, 'Turn off the TV and come here. It's time to set the table. If you don't come straight away, you will 'stand to decide' that you will.' *(Step 2 – Warning)*

No response and no move from Sarah to turn off the TV.

Jo goes in immediately, points to the place in the kitchen where she is to stand facing the wall. She says, 'Go over there right now'. Sarah does. Jo adds, 'Now you stand there until you decide to turn off the TV and start your job. Let me know when you have decided'. The TV is out of sight. *(Step 3 – Standing with a task)*

Sarah, her lower lip out in a pout, swings her hips and looks uncooperative. From the stove where she is cooking, Jo says, 'Doing that will only keep you there longer. Feel your feet on the ground, calm down and decide to do what I've told you. The sooner you do, the sooner you will be away from the wall'. (Jo is getting her more grounded.)

'But I want to watch the TV,' Sarah whines at her mother.

'Well you are not going to watch any more just now, because it's time for you to set the table. And suffering about it will not make the job go away. So stand there quietly, and decide to do what I have said.' She pauses to let that sink in, then adds, 'And next time you talk to me, talk in a normal voice'. Jo hopes that Sarah will decide easily today. She's had a long day and doesn't want a long struggle with Sarah. But she steels herself for it, just in case. She knows from experience that trying to get around these things only drags the hassling out for hours.

On this occasion, Jo is pleasantly surprised to hear Sarah speaking in a perfectly normal voice. 'Okay, Mum. I've decided.' *(Step 4 – Decision)*

'Good, ' says Jo, 'what have you decided?' *(Step 5 – Resolution begins here)*

'I'll turn off the TV and set the table.'

'That's right', says Jo, adding, 'You are to do what I tell you the first time I tell you. Will you do that from now on?' Jo is taking the opportunity to reinforce a useful parent message.

'Yes, Mum.' And Sarah goes in, turns off the TV and returns to begin setting the table. Both of them feel very good about the process and chat happily as she does.

## Reactions from parents

- 'It's fantastic. I used to feel desperate for something that would work. Now I've got it.'
- 'I feel I'm in control again. My kid doesn't run the show any more.'
- 'My children were out of control before I discovered "standing to decide".'
- 'I used to hit my kids and I don't any more. We all feel better.'
- 'The teachers have asked me what the miracle is. I said, "Standing to decide".'
- 'I couldn't get them to do things, even when I said it ten times. Now I only say it once.'
- '"Standing to decide" has given me back my life.'

## What it's good for

You can use 'standing to decide' in thousands of different ways. It is a magnificent teaching tool. Your imagination is the only limit. Here is a short list. Use it:

- to get obedience ('I'll do what you've told me.')
- to deal with resistance ('I'll stop fighting with you and do what I have to.')
- to get their attention ('I'll listen when you talk to me.')
- to stop the action and get them thinking ('I was getting angry and I wasn't thinking clearly about what I could do.')
- to change behaviour ('I'll look at you when you talk to me and I'll talk normally to you.')
- to focus attention ('I'll concentrate on what I'm doing so I don't knock things off the sink.')
- to get grounded ('I'll stay aware of my feelings and what's happening around me, so I stay steady and think.')
- to teach them to think about their feelings ('I just wanted to run away, I was so scared. Now I know what I can do next time.')
- to get a decision ('I'll make my bed first, then I'll sweep the floor.')
- to accept situations as they are ('I don't like it, and I accept that I can't go to Bill's.')
- as a timed consequence ('I don't like standing here for half an hour every time I forget, so I'll remember from now on.')
- to shift discomfort to them ('I want to be playing and don't want to be "standing to decide", so I'll do what you said.')
- to take responsibility ('I'll remember to take my washing to the laundry from now on without you reminding me.')
- to increase their strength and confidence ('I didn't want to do it, but now I've thought about it, I realise I can do lots, even when I'm scared. And you said you'd help, too.')

# Introducing the technique

We prefer to start as early as possible. And we do it when children are about eighteen months old. Naturally at that age, we need to start very simply and increase the demands only very gradually. It is usually a very light and easy process at this age.

## How to do it

Here are some guidelines for introducing eighteen-month- to two-year-olds to the process.

- We choose a wall in each room that we will use consistently.
- We take them through the process very simply at a time that they are calm and alert.
- From then on we take them to the selected wall whenever the need arises
- These are the places we go for 'little talks'.
- When they start to act in ways that we want them to change, we take them to the wall, with the statement, 'Come over here and talk to me'.
- Don't wait for them to come to you, because they are very young: take them by the hand and go with them immediately.
- Face them to the wall for about two to five seconds, then turn them around and talk to them, saying, for example, 'Right now you have to drink your milk. Are you going to drink it?' 'Yes.' 'All right, come away and do it.' And we walk them to the milk and hand it to them.

This approach puts them through the sequence easily and they generally adapt quickly to the routine. You might also say at times when you are introducing the process, 'From now on you will "stand to decide" like this when I want you to learn something or change something'. They will not understand fully what you are saying at this point, but saying it lays a foundation for future understanding.

With older children from the age of three to ten, we explain what we are going to do in simple terms that they will understand. Choose a time when they are calm or relatively calm. It is often helpful to take them through the process step by step, just as a trial. Then they know what to do because they have done it. This is easier than trying to get them used to it for the first time when they are upset about things.

With adolescents we would usually use other forms of consequence, like withdrawal of privileges or restricting freedom, rather than introduce them to 'standing to decide'. It is well worth noting, however, that if you have used 'standing to decide' when they were young, dealing with things in adolescence is generally much easier. They automatically use the process internally when they are older and become more amenable to all forms of guidance and discipline.

## How easy is it to use?

Most children take to the process very easily. Most of them also resist and struggle at times. Their resistance is not a sign that we should stop, however. 'Standing to decide' is a means of dealing with resistance. And one thing to remember is that it makes them more self-sufficient. One mother said:

> 'I used to be worried that I would squash my kids' independence. But I was wrong. They have all become stronger and lovelier, not weaker.'

The children themselves show us the value of the process. Even apart from how much more easily and quickly they learn, they do some surprising things. Quite often parents walk into a room to find their younger children standing docilely against the wall. When asked what they are doing there, the children say, 'Oh I just spilled some milk and I came here to decide to be careful', or 'I was upset because I broke dolly and wanted to calm down'. At other times, we find them putting their dolls and teddy bears against the wall, going through the instructions that we usually give to them.

These lovely signs show that they are learning, and that they are actively applying what they are learning, because they find it helpful. When a bit older, it is quite common for children to chat together as if they are members of a special 'stand to decide' club. If you listen, you will hear some wonderful stories. The best story we heard was from a seven-year-old whose mother stopped hitting him when he misbehaved and started using the process. He said with exultation, 'Oh this "standing to decide" stuff doesn't work with me at all. Whenever Mum tells me to do something or "stand to decide", I just do it!'

## A natural life process

'Standing to decide' is a natural life process. Life itself repeatedly confronts us with things that we need to learn and to resolve, until we learn or resolve them. 'Standing to decide' trains children in the same way as life will. But unlike life, which does not filter consequences, we can control the consequences and interpret them so our children can manage them and learn from them. This protected version of learning some of life's harder lessons is preparation for the real thing.

# Loving or not loving

As you discipline a child, he or she might change the subject by saying, 'Do you still love me?' or 'You don't love me any more', or 'Why don't you love me?' You are supposed to feel guilty and get trapped into reassuring the child instead of pressing on.

You have an alternative. You say, 'I do love you, but that's not what we're talking about right now'.

Then you give him or her an instruction about what to do: 'Tell me why you didn't do the dishes', 'Answer my question', 'Go and do X right now', 'Decide that you are going to do Y from now on'.

# Guidelines

The following guidelines have helped many parents get started. You may find it helpful to keep coming back to these as you learn the process.

*Remember the goal.* The goal of 'standing to decide' is for our children to learn to manage whatever stimulated us to use the process. As we manage them through to the resolution, they learn what to do. They also learn that resolution is possible. By contrast, if we walk out and leave them handling something that they cannot handle alone, then our actions become part of what they will do within themselves. Similarly, if we abuse, or rant, or rave at them, then that is what they will have inside.

*Resolution and completion are obvious.* Two definite events accompany a real end to the process. First, our children will do what they were expected to do. Second, both we and they will feel resolved and have a sense of delighted completion. Even if the process was very upsetting and disturbing at the time, we will feel like celebrating.

*Incomplete resolution is also obvious.* When children act up again very quickly after we have released them, we have stopped too quickly. Because they did not get enough the first time, we will need to repeat the process and complete it. They may need more passion from us during the process than we used the first time. Children frequently understand more from feelings than from words. So expressing what we feel is often helpful at any stage during the process. When telling our child to 'stand to decide' again, we could say, 'You just decided to do such and such and you haven't. Go over there, stand there and decide to do it right now. I feel … (angry, frustrated, disappointed, scared, sad etc.) that you did not do what you said you would'.

*The task must be possible.* The only way the process will work completely is if our children *have the ability* to do what we tell them to do. If the tasks we set them are beyond them, then we are violating or abusing them. Similarly, accepting proposals from our children that are beyond them is also abusive. ('I'll do all my homework in five minutes' – when we know it will take at least an hour.) We need to use common sense. Making the tasks we set simple and related to the issues at hand will usually ensure that we do this.

*Keep track of time.* Very young children should only 'stand to decide' for a few minutes. The attention span of young children is not long enough for them to benefit from longer periods. As they get older, however, children may spend half an hour, an hour, or more, before they resolve some issues. As the time extends, stay alert. Children taking a long time may be caught in an unproductive inner loop. Changing the scene can help with this. We can tell them to do something different that will break the inner patterns and refresh their thinking: 'Go and wash your face', 'Walk around the garden and come straight back', or 'Run upstairs and get me such and such'. If you do this, it is most important that they go straight back to standing when they return, and that they complete the task as originally set.

*Alternatives to standing sometimes work better.* With some children, getting them to sit on hard-based chairs is better than standing. Children who go passive, or slump to the floor, often respond better to running or 'being run' (hand in hand with us while they are young). We can get them to run around the backyard, or up and down the stairs.

*It is not supposed to be comfortable.* Using an uncomfortable process helps to shift motivation to inside the children, rather than leaving it in us. The discomfort encourages them to complete the task. They say, 'I don't like it here (doing this)'. We reply, 'I'm glad. I don't want you to like it. I want you away from there, enjoying yourself. You can stop standing there as soon as you do what I've told you to do'. Also, choose a location where they cannot see very much, so that distractions are reduced to a minimum. The point is for them to concentrate on the tasks we set them.

*'Time out' in a bedroom may not work well.* Some children love going to their rooms, because they have plenty to entertain them there and they are away from our pressure on them to do what they have been told to do. Also, by sending them away, we teach them internally to send their own problems away until they somehow come up with a solution without help. Having them in the room with us deals with these outcomes.

*If they get upset during the process, get them to concentrate on grounding to take care of the upset.* This will help them manage their feelings and keep them thinking as well.

*Keep going until the process is finished.* When we persist until they are finished, we teach our children to persist until they finish things, too. If we don't persist, they can learn unhelpful things like: 'Nothing gets worked out in the end', or 'All I have to do is hold out for long enough and they will give up'. We want them to make more helpful decisions than these.

*The way they act at the end is significant.* During the *decision* and *resolution* steps, they need to talk in normal, adequate voices with matching postures. We also expect sustained eye contact, although not 100 percent of the time. Expressing their feelings about issues is fine, but doing it at or against anyone is not. Any suffering, petulance, seductiveness, cuteness, inadequacy, nastiness, or unpleasantness are signs that the issue is not resolved. Any tendency to act like a Rescuer, Persecutor or Victim is something to confront. All behaviour like this signals incomplete acceptance and lack of resolution in our children. If we 'fall for it', we will know soon enough. Almost immediately, they will repeat what they did before, and we will have to repeat the whole sequence.

*Take care if physical holding is necessary.* Some children understandably don't want to stand against a blank wall, a fence or tree, or facing a corner. They want to get away and keep doing what they like. To deal with this, we need to hold them where we have told them to stay. We do this firmly, carefully and protectively, so we don't hurt them.

**Some children need the physical struggle of being held in position, to learn what they need to learn.** Children learn many things physically. Self-control is one of these. Many children learn to control themselves, through being controlled physically by others. They use the external control as a physical base from which to control **themselves**. 'Standing to decide' gives us an opportunity to do this with them. If our children are already too big for one of us to manage at the point we begin using the process, we might need both of us there for a while.

Here is a very extreme example that highlights what some children will do and the power of persisting.

*Harry was an unhappy five-year-old. His mother was a lone parent who could not control him. He would not do anything she told him. He was so violent and uncontrolled at school that he was under threat of expulsion. Elizabeth discussed 'standing to decide' in front of him with his mother. Immediately after she finished, he did something extremely provocative. Elizabeth turned and asked his mother if she would like to use 'standing to decide' to deal with it. She agreed. Harry was told to talk politely to his mother and would not. For the next three hours, this boy yelled and screamed in rage, struggled against their hold on him and tried to hurt them. They persisted until he calmed down, accepted what he had to do, spoke to his mother politely and agreed to do what he was told in future. The next day his mother rang in tears of relief to say that Harry was completely transformed. A week later, she rang again to say that the school were astonished at the transformation in him. He was calm, attentive, responsive and happy. His happiness was the most obvious change to everyone. By controlling him physically, he had learnt to manage himself.*

**Our strength helps them develop the strength to manage themselves.** When our children struggle with us over discipline, the strength of the struggle shows us the strength of their need of us. They need us to join with them with the same strength. If they are dealing with a sledgehammer inside, using a feather outside will not help; if they are shouting inside, a whispered or quiet response from us will barely be heard.

**Make appropriate allowances for tiredness or illness.** It is appropriate to act with more leniency when the children are tired or ill. But making the allowance does not gives them permission to act in unpleasant or difficult ways when they are tired or sick.

*Useful one-liners . . .*

### Interrupting the drama

You have a child who really makes a meal of inadequacy, or gets very worked up.

You say humorously – not nastily, **'Oh it must be worse than that'**, or **'I bet you could be even more convincing, if you shouted some more/produced more tears/spoke even more quietly so it's completely impossible to hear you'.** When we do this well, they will often laugh with us and become more communicative. You need to choose your timing and do this only with children over about seven years of age.

# Chapter 4

# Knowing when and how to act

As parents, we are often in the position of wondering whether we should or should not do something. Also, not uncommonly, we simply don't know what to do: 'Should I leave them to themselves?'; 'Maybe it will be all right'; 'It'll only create hassles'; 'I'm worried, but maybe I'm mistaken.'

# Who takes the initiative?

Let's take a look at what we do with our children from the point of view of initiative. Knowing who is taking the initiative can help a lot when we need to decide what to do. It helps us answer questions such as:

- Do I need to take the initiative and act right now?
- Is it best just to get on with things as they are?
- Is it effective for me just to wait and react when the children do something?

What we do is to divide how we are parenting into three types:
1. In *proactive parenting* we take the initiative.
2. In *active parenting* initiative is evenly balanced between ourselves and our children.
3. In *reactive parenting* our children have the initiative.

Fairly obviously, good parenting involves all three types. With a balance of the three, we can more easily shape our children's talents and abilities at the same time as we support their uniqueness. So let's explore them so you can understand the way each contributes to our children.

*Proactive parenting* is most helpful when we need to set the agenda. Our images, feelings or senses of how we want our children to turn out, prompt us to guide them actively in those directions. We provide them with the opportunities they need, we make suggestions, we keep some level of pressure on them until they learn. We parent like this when our children would not learn what is important without us introducing and following through with the necessary lessons. For example, you want your child to be physically fit, so you organise involvement in sports and other physical activities; or you want your child to discuss things intelligently, so you talk at every opportunity and encourage wide-ranging reading.

*Active parenting* is most helpful when we simply need to get on with the job of dealing with day-to-day events. Much parenting involves this. We get on with paying bills, doing the washing, wiping away tears, buying school books, celebrating successes, discussing ways of doing things and having fun.

*Reactive parenting* is most helpful when we are responding to our children's initiatives. They do something and we get them to change what they are doing, because it needs rebalancing or correcting. During this kind of parenting, the children's actions set the agenda and we respond to them. For example, our children spend too much time watching TV, or don't spend enough time with friends, or argue a lot, or do not pay attention when others are talking to them, or hit others. At these times we will respond, deliberately shaping our responses so that they get the suggestions and corrections they need from us.

> Act on the basis of what your children need. Their approval does not show us that we are right or wrong.

We can, however, parent too much in any of these ways. Overdoing any of them can create problems.

Too much *proactive parenting* can result in children who overemphasise the importance of other people's opinions and actions. They can lose a sense of what is important to themselves. At the same time, we can become dulled to their needs and desires, because we are so preoccupied with our own agendas. Too much *proactive parenting* can produce:

- children with other natural talents, who choose jobs that they think will please their parents;
- people who 'never' relax, because they 'always' had chores to do when growing up, rarely getting the chance to please and entertain themselves;
- grown-ups who 'stop knowing' what they hope for, think and feel while talking to others, because they were so overloaded as children by what their parents hoped, thought and felt.

With too much *active parenting*, we can get so preoccupied by the day-to-day events of our children's lives, that we don't pay enough attention to the important general issues affecting them. The bills get paid, many household chores get done, the squabbles and fights get dealt with, but overall outcomes are forgotten or not even noticed. In other words, everyday detail is noticed, while the general is forgotten or ignored. Too much *active parenting* can produce:

- a young person, who gets to the end of school and still cannot read, because she managed to 'become invisible' in class and won't talk about it at home;
- a child who has no friends and no-one has noticed, because parents spend most time correcting her 'faults';
- a primary school where no programs encourage physical exercise, because they are overbusy with classroom work.

Too much *reactive parenting* can mean that we unintentionally allow our children to determine what gets the attention. Attention is given to what they do, while other things are ignored. We wait for events to occur before taking action. Planning ahead is rare. We can easily forget important things. Too much *reactive parenting* can mean:

- you wait until you run out of food before doing the shopping;
- you miss the opportunity of a school camp by not sending in the application on time;
- you spend most time dealing with arguments and lose sight of the importance of sharing enjoyment;
- you prevent children from working easily and reliably as adults by not having trained them to contribute to the household every day when they were children.

Staying aware of the value of each of these three ways of acting can prompt us to do some important things and help us keep an overall balance in what we do.

> If in doubt about how to act, do something that you hope will help. Inactivity implies that we agree with what we are witnessing. Far better to repent after the event for having done too much, than to regret not having done enough.

# Safety first

Safety is fundamentally important at all times. To ensure our children survive to become healthy, happy and fulfilled adults, we need to stay alert for and deal with real threats. In all situations, safety is the highest priority. Safety applies at all ages.

All events that could cause death or significant harm have to be dealt with. They may be external threats, or threats posed by the children's own risk-taking behaviour. Be alert to:

- the traffic on the roads and in car parks
- underwater swimming hazards
- threatening-looking dogs or other animals
- depression in a child or young person
- dangerous driving
- train surfing

> Whenever a threat occurs, you need to do whatever is necessary to deal with it effectively.

We need to be on the alert always. Keeping our children safe requires that we move in and deal effectively with any potential or actual threats. Also, we need to make teaching our children to keep themselves safe a high priority.

## Safety checklist

Can it:

| | | |
|---|---|---|
| be swallowed | drown | bruise |
| cut | damage | hurt |
| burn | break | injure |
| trip | chill | suffocate |
| poison | electrocute | bite |
| choke | tear | |

If the answer is 'yes' to any of these, then we need to remove the danger, or protect our children from it.

# Imagining the future

Casting our thinking forward into the future gives wonderful guidance about what to do now. When we understand this, either our goals or our children's behaviour can give us reasons to act.

## Our goals

The moment we know how we want our children to turn out, many decisions about what to do with them become obvious. So, if you have not already done it, give some thought to the kinds of people you want your children to turn into. Parents can have lots of fun discussing this.

When we recommend thinking about children like this, we suggest you consider general ideas, not specific programs. For example, we want children to have happy, prosperous lives, in which they contribute to the world in some way that is fulfilling for themselves; we want them to be caring, intelligent, playful, assertive, powerful, sensitive and aware people.

*Once you have even a general idea of how you want your children to turn out, do your best to fashion them accordingly.* Use your ideas to measure them. This approach can easily guide you to when you need to act.

- If what they are doing is consistent with your ideas, then encourage them to do more of it.
- If what they do is inconsistent, then discourage them from doing it again.
- If what they do is not quite on track or inconsistent, you guide them to act differently.

Here are a few examples.

- Your young children remember names of visitors, or things you have said to them from several days before. Wanting them to develop good memories, you congratulate them.
- Primary school children are often unpleasant to each other. By actively encouraging them to care about each other, we can help them learn to live very differently with others.

- Babies often turn away and bury their heads in their parents' necks. You can say, 'Oh he's/she's shy', if you want a shy adult. For a confident adult, turn yourself around, or gently turn the child around for a full view.

Clarify what kinds of adults you want your children to become. Then, every day, actively encourage them towards this outcome.

- The pressure of school work mounts on your adolescent children. You want them to have the chance of tertiary education. Helping them cope with the pressure and insisting that they do the necessary work, will help them with this. Allowing them to give up, or doing it for them may well cut off the chance completely.

## Our children's behaviour

Taking our children's behaviour as the reference is often equally powerful. A simple approach works with any incident.

*We imagine that our children are twenty years older and are acting in the same way as they do now.*

As we imagine this, we ask ourselves, 'How would I react to adults doing this?' If we like the prospect, then we encourage our children to keep doing it. If we don't like it, or could foresee problems with it, then we do something to change what our children are doing.

- A 40-year-old university lecturer was at a meeting. When thwarted during the meeting, she threw herself down, drummed her heels and her hands on the floor, and screamed in a full tantrum. It took little imagination to work out what she was allowed to do from about two years of age.

Our experience shows us repeatedly that adult patterns of feeling, thinking, behaving and understanding often come directly from the past.

- A boy pushes through people blocking access to a door, intent on his own goal of getting to the food first. Just imagine this behaviour when he is behind the wheel of a car.

- In response to people and events cutting across his plans, a boy dissolves into tears of frustration and acts helplessly in a manner that is out of proportion to the events. Can you foresee how he'll behave when he is grown up?
- When faced with challenging people, your children try to find out what is upsetting others, identify what is important to them and act in ways that help to calm things down and solve any problems. Do you want them doing this when they are older?

## Remember they are still children

Obviously, our children are not adults. Just as obviously, they are not yet fully capable of doing things as adults do them. We need to stay aware of this as we act and ensure that we set reasonable expectations of our children that match their age.

- The boy can be stopped at the door, or brought back through it, expected to apologise for having pushed people and expected to wait until others have gone through first.
- The child prone to upsets can be encouraged to accept such inevitable events calmly. His parents may deliberately interfere in his plans at times, to help him learn. This gets him used to the process in protected places.
- Parents may encourage the clear-thinking, problem-solving children by complimenting them on their approaches. Further discussion may help to expand their already developing abilities.

### A simple exercise

How on track are your kids at the moment? If you project forward twenty years, will you be happy for your children to act and live as they now do? Think about what you like and don't like about what they are doing. Starting with one or two of each type of behaviour, decide what you can do to further encourage what you like, and what you can do to change what you don't like. Make a decision to do at least one thing a day in both areas.

# Meeting provocations

Children often deliberately provoke us. *When they are provocative, usually our best response is to deal directly with the provocations.*

## Reasons for acting

*Their provocations are deliberate, though possibly unconscious, attempts to get the guidance that they need from us.* When they have gaps in what they need to cope, they will often provoke us to help them fill the gaps. Also, when what they have got is not working well for them, they may provoke us to help them learn to manage themselves differently. They are provoking us to fill gaps and to help them better to learn to control and channel their feelings and other experiences.

## Three provocations for us to act on
They put themselves or others at risk.
They break known rules inside or outside their homes.
They do things that create problems for themselves or others.

*When what they do is prompted by these needs, the only way of stopping them is to act decisively and effectively.* If we don't, they will keep escalating the seriousness of what they do, until we do. This is very important to understand. They act more and more outrageously so that we will stop them, not so we will leave them to it. Once stopped, we can engage them in learning to act differently.

These kinds of escalations can occur over months or years, which can dull some parents' awareness of what is occurring.

- The boy, who at two would not do what his mother said, by three was hitting her, by four was kicking and biting her, and by fourteen knocked her unconscious and left her on the floor.

- The girl, who was quiet as a little girl, began running to her room to hide and cry when upset at seven, took an overdose at fifteen.
- The girl, who started lying to solve problems at seven and would not change, added stealing to her repertoire at about nine, played truant frequently at thirteen, stole cars at sixteen and robbed a bank at twenty-one.

When provoking us to act from a need for learning, they will only stop when they have learnt.

Trying to ignore or step around their provocations only leads to more serious and stimulating provocations.

They need us to stop them, using whatever vigour it takes to do so.

*Children doing this kind of thing often have parents who have not given them enough limits in other areas.* As the children escalate, they are trying to find something that will stir us enough to say, 'No. Stop doing that', or 'Not like that, like this'. Another ingredient is also important. They want us to enforce what we have said. They know in their bones that they need controlling by others, so they can learn to guide or control themselves. But they cannot do it for themselves. Fortunately, most children manage to find our sensitive spots eventually and so get us to set the limits they need. Tactics include:

- doing damage to a favourite possession;
- a maths teacher's daughter threatening to give up maths at school;
- the son of a probation officer of juveniles breaking the law and ends up in court in front of his father's friends;
- the daughter of an inflexible minister of religion getting pregnant at sixteen.

## When parents don't act

Unfortunately, some children don't manage to stir their parents into action. This leaves it up to others to take care of the consequences. Teachers are very involved in this job. When parents, teachers and interested adults all fail to act, our children often get what they need from the police, ambulance, fire brigade, the prison system, psychiatric hospitals or armed forces.

Our shared view is that much social turmoil, and acting out in public, are attempts by people, who were not guided or limited enough at home, to get that guidance and those limits outside the home. We include much drug-taking, leaving home too early, fighting and demonstrating on the streets, crime and destruction of property. Many discussions with adults who did this kind of thing when young have told us remarkably similar stories.

- One side of it is: 'My parents never stopped me when I was a kid. I realise now that I needed them to stop me.'
- Another side is: 'I didn't like my parents limiting me, but in another way I knew they were right and I was relieved.'

### What works

When questioned by her mother, one young woman explained why she had never even experimented with drugs. She said, 'I always knew you and Dad were there for me. You encouraged me when I needed it and I could feel your hands on the reins when I needed correction. Feeling secure in your presence, I did not need to provoke you by using drugs and doing other things, the way a lot of my friends did. I already knew you cared'.

# Choosing when to struggle

Children need to struggle as part of growing up. We have already mentioned in several places the way this works. When our children struggle with us, they want us 'to win', not 'to lose'. It is our guiding strength that they are after, and they get it from the struggle. (You will see much more on this in *ParentCraft*, Chapter 20, 'Four births, four bonds'.)

> Struggle is a normal and important part of raising children.

As you think about your children's struggles, you will almost certainly notice something very obvious about them. When struggle is part of their learning, it doesn't much matter what we do, they will keep struggling. There is no way around the struggle, if we want our children to learn. This understanding leads to a wonderfully simple guideline for us. *Since the struggle is what is important, not so much what they are struggling about, we can choose when to struggle with them.*

In other words, a little *proactive parenting* is the solution. Instead of waiting on our children 'to pick the next fight', we do some choosing about when it will be and what it will be over, too. We will generally feel much better if we exercise some level of choice over things.

All sorts of issues are available in our daily lives, including expecting them to do household jobs. And we can't go wrong. If they struggle over doing something reasonable and we struggle with them to ensure they do it, then we are on the right track. They get the struggle they need. If they don't struggle and do as requested or expected, they contribute to the household. And everyone benefits from their contributions. You can:

- expect them to put their clothes away, do the dishes properly, or make their beds daily;

- stop them swearing at you and each other;
- ensure brothers and sisters talk to each other respectfully;
- get them to go to bed at the right time;
- insist on truth and keeping commitments.

These are much easier issues to deal with than the more serious things they are likely to do if we don't give them the struggles they need. Also, remember a simple thing. Children and young people know that they need discipline. While they may fight our attempts to provide it, they are not fighting 'to win'. They are fighting so we will 'win', because with our 'victory' they learn what they need. In the end, of course, they realise that it never was a fight over who was going to win or lose. (Please understand that we assume that your parenting is appropriate and not abusive or violating. See Chapter 1, 'Parenting with love', Chapter 2, 'The discipline sequence', and Chapter 3, 'Standing to decide' for more information on how we approach this.)

## John's rescue mission

John was at a loss about what to do with his fourteen year-old daughter, Mary. She had started to challenge him very strongly several months before. Then one night she didn't arrive home as arranged. Uncertain of the right thing to do, he went to look for her to bring her home.

He found her with a group of friends in a park watching a concert. In a low voice, he said to her, 'If you come quietly with me now, we can talk about this at home. If you don't come with me immediately, I will make a public spectacle of you.'

She didn't, so he did.

Mary was astonished at her father's behaviour. But for the first time in months of struggling and hassling, she 'really heard' what he had to say. Interestingly, she relaxed inside rather than the opposite, and was a model citizen at home for several weeks.

John acted precisely as Mary needed him to, right when she needed it.

# Supporting talents

*Support your children's natural inclinations and expressiveness as much as is reasonable.* Notice what they like doing and where their talents are. Then do what you can to provide opportunities for them to develop in these areas. Examples are:

- one little girl played with many different things and obviously loved drawing and painting;
- from when he could walk, a boy showed great prowess with bats and balls of all kinds;
- another child began counting, measuring, numbering and keeping track of physical things from the moment he could talk.

If you are unclear what is important to your children, ask them. They can tell you directly. Parents can often make the mistake of trying to work things out themselves. But this wastes much time and can lead to significant mistakes when we are wrong. Once they can talk, talk to them. Ask questions and listen intently to their answers.

- What do you want to do?
- What do you need?
- How would you go about doing this?
- Why did you do that?
- What did you think would happen when you did that?
- If you could have anything you needed, what would it be?

## Go to the horse's mouth

Children can surprise us with their maturity, perceptiveness, insight and understanding. They can also startle us with their levels of confusion, misunderstanding and ignorance. In either event, we are better off knowing, and they can be better off for the discussions we have with them as we find out.

# Dealing with suicidal children

Children can become very dejected at times and may become suicidal. Our actions at these times need to be direct, clear, effective and sustained. Suicidal or potentially suicidal children and young people are at risk and need immediate and effective adult help. We do not need special training to recognise the problem and act effectively.

Children as young as five or six may consider killing themselves and it is important to take these threats seriously.

## Warning signs

Things to watch for include actual suicide attempts, threats to do it, talking about dying or not wanting to live, extreme acting out or withdrawal, depression, sustained isolation, stopping eating. We need to be particularly alert after a significant loss (of a parent, sibling, friend, pet), parental divorce, family breakdown, or during intense personal emotional crises. Most of these signs and situations do not automatically mean a child will be suicidal; however, they are definitely signs to us that we need to do something.

## Things to do

We can all do a great deal to help. And what we do could save a life. Things to do when you think children are at risk:

- reach out and express your concern
- discuss their issues and feelings openly and directly
- avoid avoiding the issue
- ensure their safety by having someone with them until help arrives
- attempt to get a life contract and/or no-suicide contract
- remove all likely instruments: pills, knives, razor blades, guns, poisons etc.
- block access to any dangerous places: cliffs, high windows, roads, kitchen drawers etc.
- contact emergency services – police, ambulance – if necessary
- link them to professional help and follow up until the link is made
- follow up again after a while to make sure everything is working out

## Agreements to live

Once physically safe, we can ask the children or young people to make special agreements with us. These help us both to assess how at risk they are and to secure their safety. The ease with which they make the agreements is the measure: the easier it is, the safer they are.

## Life contract

I am living (will live) a happy and full life, and promote the same in others.

## No-suicide contract

I will not kill myself nor harm myself in any way, either accidentally or on purpose, nor will I allow anyone else to do it for me.

## How to make the agreements

These are simple statements that commit children and young people to staying alive. They can be made with or without a time-limit. The way to do it is to keep on getting the children or young people to repeat the words until they say them with real conviction.

We also ask that they make the contracts forever. If they are reluctant to do this, we ask them what the longest time is that they are sure they will keep them. This might be five minutes, an hour, a day, several days, a week, a month, several months, a year or more.

Any time limit is specified as part of the agreements. We also get them to agree to contact us again before the specified time limit expires. 'I will keep this agreement for ... And I will contact you at ...' To add extra security, we get them to agree to contact us at any other time that they think they are becoming unsure about keeping the agreements. Then we **must** make sure that we get the child to remake the contracts again **before** the time expires.

We also need to make sure we are available for contact, should they need to call on us. If we don't think we have the capacity to do this, or we are unwilling or unavailable to be contacted, then it is most important that we get someone else to take over this part of the process. (See Chapter 8, 'Developing self-esteem' for more on what we can do to help children and young people in this fix.)

# Chapter 5

# Communicating clearly

Life is much simpler for parents when we communicate clearly with our children. Naturally, most of us want to make things as easy as we can. A lot of our difficulties arise from what we say and the way we say it. Fortunately, several basic secrets that help to ensure clear communication are remarkably simple and easy to use, and many parents have found that they make a difference. This chapter is about what children really hear when we speak to them and what we can do to ensure that they get the messages we want them to get.

# What children really hear

As adults, we usually know what we and others mean. Life experience has taught us the significance of what they say and do. Children, particularly the younger ones, do not have our experience, however. What they make out of what we are trying to get across to them is often very different from what we intend. Take three examples.

- After playing with friends, seven-year-old Vito came inside at dusk. His mother caught sight of him with mud from head to foot. She said, 'Go straight to the laundry and put everything you are wearing in the washing machine'. And this is what he did. Everything went into the machine: shirt, pants, underclothes, socks, boots and watch. He did precisely what he was told to do.

- Anne's mother wanted her to prepare for the evening meal. Anne was four years old. Her mother said, 'I want you to pick up your toys.' Anne nodded as she said this and then did nothing about her toys. When she was reprimanded for not picking up her toys, she looked very confused and got upset. Anne did not know that, by '*I want you* to pick up your toys', her mother meant, '*Pick up* your toys'. To Anne, her mother had simply said something interesting.

- Wendy was having a great struggle with Sam, her nine-month-old boy. A large, strong child for his age, whenever she changed his nappy, he kept rolling over and trying to crawl away from her. Wendy was very frustrated and worried that he would become uncontrollable as he got older. Ken suggested that she change Sam in front of him, so he could witness the process. As she put Sam on his back and took off his nappy, Sam quickly rolled over and tried to crawl away. Wendy said, 'Don't move'. He tried to get away even more strongly. She repeated herself, loudly, 'Don't *move!*' As before, he did his best to get away. At this point Ken said, 'Wendy, try saying, "Keep still".' Wendy immediately said, 'Keep still'. Sam stopped immediately. 'Now,' said Ken, 'put him on his back, and as you do, say, "Lie still while I change your nappy".' Wendy followed the suggestion and Sam did exactly what he was told.

Vito, Anne and Sam all did what they thought they were told to do. They did not do what their mothers intended them to do, but they did do quite literally what their mothers had said. There is a lesson in this.

To get your children to do as you want, choose your words carefully and tell them *exactly* what you want them to do.

## How this works

Young children are 'body minded'. This means that they understand the meaning of words and events physically. *The meanings of words and events are the actions and objects that go with them.* Children cannot understand in any other way, at least when they are young.

To understand anything, our children go through the motions internally. They live through it inside. Children up to the age of about four or five do this very obviously by acting out what they say as they say it. As children get older they seem to stop. However, even though they may look as though they have stopped, they still do it internally. So, in fact, do we.

### Messages for children

'You are responsible for what you say. Choose your words with care.'
'Talk in a normal/regular voice, stop suffering/whining/acting cute /acting coy.'
'Say what you want directly. You won't always get it then, but at least we will know what you want.'

# Getting messages across

The first tip we have relates to body-mindedness. It is to put into words, pictures and action exactly what you want your children to do. All the suggestions that follow involve doing this. They can make all sorts of situations with our children very much easier, including the challenging job of getting them to do what we want quickly and easily.

## Choose your words carefully

This could be the one piece of advice that makes most difference in your home. You can powerfully influence the lightness, happiness, ease and harmony there and in your life generally. Many parents have confirmed this. So look, listen and follow through!

*Choose your words according to their literal and concrete meaning.* You will almost certainly notice all sorts of things become much easier if you do. We can influence the moods and orientations of our children directly and we can get them to do the things that are important much more easily and cooperatively. Let's look at each in turn.

### *Influencing moods*

Remembering that children act out the literal meaning of the words we use, we can program them with our words. When we want our children to experience and think about love, success, happiness, enjoying themselves, calming down, thinking clearly, solving problems, cooperating, cheering up and many other things, we simply use those exact words. Experiment. Next time your children are with you, decide how you would like them to feel. Then as you talk, start to use the words that go with those feelings. Every time you do, you will stimulate your children and yourself to have those precise experiences. After very little time you are likely to notice a shift towards what you are saying.

This has general and specific value. Take our families. We can monitor the words we usually use as we talk to each other. Knowing that we are all acting out the meanings of them, we can assess the influence these words are having. We can use this influence, simply by changing the words we use. We have seen families shift their overall atmospheres within hours of starting this process. Each member can become a monitor of everyone else to help make the changes. It can be a lot of fun. For example, imagine the difference between acting out, 'I'm sick and tired of telling you ...', and 'I want you to do this right now'.

Specific value lies in our responses to each other's needs. Selecting our words can make us much more sensitive, effective and creative.

- Andrea walks in crying. 'I'm very upset', she says. (This intensifies her upset, which could be a good thing at this stage.)

    Mother says, 'Oh you poor thing, you look as though your world is about to end. Come over here and tell me about it'. (Notice the 'poor thing' and 'your world is about to end'. Is this what we want Andrea acting out?)

    Andrea cries some more and struggles to say, 'I'm just so hopeless, everyone hates me. I'll never have any friends'. (All of this is probably a real expression of her feelings, but not true in fact, or at least not destined to stay true.)

    Mother caresses her and says, 'You're not hopeless, everyone doesn't hate you. I'm sure you have lots of friends'. (The first two statements are not helpful, although intended to show sympathy. Andrea acts out 'so hopeless', and 'hate you'. Mother's last statement is better. Acting out 'have lots of friends' will be good for her, although Andrea may not be quite ready to hear this, yet.)

Now let's look at a different set of responses.

- Andrea walks in crying. 'I'm very upset,' she says.

    Mother says, 'Oh dear, come over here and talk to me about it. I'm sure we can work something out. What's going on? You certainly don't look happy.' (She plants a seed about working things out and requests more information. Then she gives her an internal nudge in the direction of feeling better by using the word 'happy'.)

Andrea, still upset, walks across to her mother and says, 'I'm just so hopeless, everyone hates me. I'll never have any friends'.

Mother, holding her hands, says, 'Sometimes when we don't feel happy, we imagine things are not nearly as good as they actually are. Usually, when we feel better, we realise that things are better than we thought'. (Note the selection of words and phrases like 'feel happy', 'nearly as good as', 'feel better', and 'better than we thought'. All of these, when acted out will help Andrea start to appreciate things differently.)

'Oh it's all right for *you*, *you've* got plenty of friends.' Andrea is now both angry and sad. (This is actually a step forward. She is more assertive and is using words like 'plenty of friends'.)

'That's not the point, Andrea. The main point is that you don't feel as if *you* have friends. You don't like yourself much at the moment and we need to work out what to do about it. Let's talk about it. There are solutions to all problems.' (Mother is still programming her and leading her both to face herself and to think practically about what to do.)

## Changing behaviour with clear instructions

Many parents find their children are much more responsive to doing what they are told, when they are told what to do, rather than what not to do. Why they are, is very obvious, when we remember that children act out literally what we say to them. Think about the literal meaning of the following examples in the table. Imagine your children acting out the actual words used and decide if your selection would be the same as ours. Note that when we give someone a negative message (don't, can't, never, not etc.) we act out the message first and only then get to not doing it. In other words, 'Don't cry', means that the person has to cry internally before not doing it.

| Expressions to use | Expressions to avoid |
| --- | --- |
| Act gently. | Don't hit. |
| Talk quietly. | Don't shout. |
| Come away, hands off. | Don't touch. |
| Relax. | Don't be scared. |
| Act intelligently. | Don't be stupid. |
| Tell the truth. | Don't lie. |
| Get out of bed. | Don't lie there. |
| Remember. | Don't forget. |
| Think clearly. | Don't be confused. |
| Go well. | 'Break a leg'. |
| Move carefully. | Don't be clumsy. |
| Act pleasantly. | Don't be nasty. |
| Walk slowly. | Don't run. |
| Obey the law. | Don't break the law. |

You will see that acting out the statements on the left will get your children to do what you intend. Many parents find that their children become much easier to manage, the moment they talk in this way. While the approach doesn't get 100 per cent success, it makes even those times when children struggle strongly against us much easier to resolve.

## Messages for children

'I don't like what you're doing and I want you to change it. So sit down, figure out what you'll do differently, then come and talk to me about it.'

# Using requests and instructions

Requests and instructions are different. Using the differences well makes dealing with our children and helping them understand what we want them to do very much easier. Let's consider the differences.

A *request* is the act of asking someone to do something. Requests usually carry a tone of politeness with them. They also include the assumption that the person is free to choose. He or she can say, 'Yes', 'No', or 'Maybe'.

An *instruction*, by contrast, is a direction or command to do something. They are usually not thought of as polite. When we give an instruction, we expect to be obeyed. People given and instruction, can still say, 'Yes', 'No', or 'Maybe', but this would require that they go against usual expectations.

We have found that children are much more confident in many ways when their parents are clear on this difference. Mixing up requests and instructions can create all sorts of unnecessary difficulties. Look at the following example. As you do, remember that children understand things literally, so a request will get them internally acting out the question, while an instruction gets them internally actually doing what we expect.

> A warder asked a prisoner, 'Will you go to your cell now please?' The prisoner replied, 'Do I have a choice?' The warder repeated himself, 'Will you go to your cell now please?' The prisoner repeated himself, too, 'Do I have a choice?' After two more repetitions, the warder became angry and put the prisoner on report.

Obviously, the question and seeming politeness were covering an instruction that had to be obeyed. The prisoner's question was appropriate under the circumstances, although perhaps not wise.

Make your requests as requests and give your instructions as instructions.

Take a quick look at the clear difference in the examples given in the table.

| Requests | Instructions |
|---|---|
| Will you go to bed now? | Go to bed now. |
| Will you eat your meal? | Eat your meal. |
| Will you come home by midnight? | Come home by midnight. |
| Will you clean up your room before tea? | Clean up your room before tea. |

## Advantages of being clear

Several compelling reasons support making clear the difference between requests and orders.

- Our children will always know when we are offering them a choice and when we are not.
- Parents who ask their children to do things, when they are not actually offering a choice, imply a shift of power to their children. This is unreal and not good for either parents or children in many situations.
- Because our children record what we do with them and use the recordings to help manage themselves, they can take in two important things from us. The first is the power to command themselves to do things. The second is the freedom to choose for themselves. If we confuse the two, so might they. If we act clearly, so might they.
- When we act assertively enough to get our children to do quickly and cleanly what we direct, we can save hours of wheedling, pleading, coaxing and hoping that our children will do what we want them to do.

## Reluctance to give orders

Even given the advantages, however, you may have qualms about instructing, ordering or telling your children what to do. Many parents react to this as harsh or bossy, or even nasty and abusive. And, while any of us can act in harsh, bossy, nasty or abusive ways, this is not an automatic part of giving an instruction. We can give instructions very mildly, even lovingly and humorously. Probably most situations allow us to do this, too.

- Said in a normal speaking voice, 'Eat your vegetables, John'.
- In a soft, mild, or even loving voice, 'Come on now. It's time for bed. Get going'. This could be said with a smile, or done with a kiss on the top of the head, or with other forms of affection.
- Loudly enough to be heard over the traffic, but still evenly and clearly, 'Come over here away from the road, Angela. It's not safe there. Come on, come here quickly'.
- Said with a laugh, 'Okay, the time has come for you to do your homework. Did you think I had forgotten? Your father isn't that forgetful yet! Go on, go and get started'.

It is all right to tell your children what to do.

## Sometimes we need to shout

When talking to our children, we do not usually need to shout, sound hard, or threaten with posture, gestures, or voice tones. Sometimes we do, however, so it is worth being prepared. This is particularly important when our children are not taking notice of us and we need something extra to get them to do so. Our intensity and noise are what we use.

- After a lot of repeated appearances at the door, we say in a firm voice, louder than usual, with perhaps a frown or two for good effect, 'I will not discuss it with you any more. Go to bed, now. Lie down and stay there. Go on – now'.
- 'You have not remembered your school notices all this week. You are to remember to give them to me every time notices are given to you. You are to give them to me the moment you get home.' All this is said very clearly, firmly (possibly

loudly) and each point is made one at a time. Then you say, 'Now what are you going to do?' (See Chapter 2, 'The discipline sequence'.)

Shouting, table-thumping and other displays of parental displeasure are valuable ways of getting attention, keeping attention and giving emotional significance to what we are saying. When we have their attention and they have got the message, we can behave normally again. Phew!

One of the wonderful things about using 'standing to decide' with children is that it removes the necessity for a lot of shouting and soothes much parental frustration. (See Chapter 3, 'Standing to decide'.)

## The power of requests

Requests are just as powerful in their own way. They offer choices to our children very clearly.

- 'Will you help me with the dishes?' gives them the freedom to say, 'Yes' or 'No'. This encourages them to think for themselves and act cooperatively or independently. And in asking the question, we are implying that we are prepared to do the dishes without their help.
- 'Will you come and see me about that tomorrow?' implies that they can, and could also come at another time, or not at all.
- 'Will you ask your mother to make the carrots I like tonight?' also implies that they don't have to do it. We are asking it as a favour.

## Politeness can be a trap

In an effort to emphasise politeness and to encourage respect, many parents add the words 'please' or 'okay' to the end of their questions.

- 'Will you drink your milk now, please?'

- 'Will you go over there and play on the carpet, please?'
- 'Will you finish your homework now, so you can get to bed early, okay?'

The words 'please' and 'okay' are supposed to act as some sort of verbal punctuation that turns the request into an instruction. The level of compulsion attached to these 'requests' varies according to the intensity in how they are said. When our children don't do what we have 'told' them to do like this, we generally become increasingly irritated and impatient. At these times, it usually becomes clear that our questions are shams. And the more forceful the emphasis that is put on the 'please' or 'okay', the more clearly the request is revealed as an instruction:

- 'Will you go to bed now, *please!?*'
- 'Will you children *please* be quiet?'

Instructions that we pretend are requests, such as these, transmit very mixed messages to our children. Here are some of the possibilities:

- 'I am telling you to do this, but I don't feel confident enough to tell you directly.'
- 'I am in charge of you, but I ask your permission before taking control of you.'
- 'I hope you will take care of me by doing what I want you to do, without me having to assert myself directly and tell you to do it.'

Remember that every one of these messages is taken in by our children and used by them to get themselves to do what they need to do in their lives. Is this the inner heritage you wish to pass on to your children? We don't, although we know people who are quite happy to do it. We can call this 'parenting from the Victim position'.

We think the best thing to do is simply to give a clear instruction as outlined above and follow through so they do as they are told. This saves lots of time and parental wear and tear.

- 'Go to bed now.'
- 'Be quiet, children.'

When you expect your children to do things and they have no choice, give them instructions. When they have a choice, as they often will, make requests of them.

# A true story

*A child had his fingers on the moving surface of an airport luggage carousel. His mother, obviously concerned about the safety of his fingers, said, 'Can you be careful of your fingers?' The child moved his fingers about two millimetres, so showing that he had heard the question. She repeated her question and got the same slight twitch of a response. The child's eyes were still down, looking attentively at the moving surface. Then she repeated it twice more. By this time over a minute had passed. Finally, she said with irritation, as if the child had not done what he was told, 'Get your hand off!' And she slapped him, not hurtfully, on the shoulder. The child, looking confused, immediately moved his hand away from danger.*

We witnessed this sequence and noticed several things.

- The mother was concerned and was trying to get her son to take proper care. We knew this because we shared her concern and were old enough to know what she intended, whereas the boy may not have understood.
- The literal meaning of her repeated question was, 'Are you able to be careful of your fingers?' This did not require much of a response from her son. 'Yes', meaning that he could be careful, or 'No', meaning that he could not.
- The child's slight physical response indicated that he had heard, but did not feel the need to respond further.
- The mother was obviously used to telling this boy to do things more than once, too, even things to do with his safety. It took four repetitions of the same question for her to act decisively. All the while, her son was trailing his fingers across the moving surface of the carousel.

- You might wonder if the boy was rebellious and just not wanting to cooperate; however, our impression was that he was absorbed in what he was doing, not rebellious.
- The moment she said clearly, 'Get your hand off!' and slapped him on the shoulder, he acted. The slap got his attention and the words said *exactly* what she wanted him to do.
- Her irritation seemed due to his unresponsiveness. However, it was only her last statement that communicated clearly what she wanted.

Our impression was that she would have been better to start where she ended: 'Get your hand off'. The boy would probably have acted immediately and the slap to get his attention may not have been necessary. This would have kept his fingers much safer, avoided the mother becoming irritated and prevented the boy feeling somewhat confused.

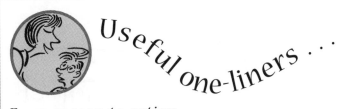

## Useful one-liners . . .

### From reason to action

A child repeatedly avoids action by seeking reasons why.

After they say 'Why?' you say, **'Because I am telling you to. Do it now'**.

### Cooling it

'Oh, you're so uncool!' our children say in an attempt to sway us to their way of thinking.

We can reply casually, **'It's okay to be hot at times'**.

# Chapter 6

# Paying active attention

This chapter is about truly knowing what is going on with our children. To do this, we need both to pay attention to them and to get them to tell us what is going on.

# How we notice our children

To pay attention to our children, we have to notice them. The simplest thing to remember about attention is that we have five senses. This gives us five ways of knowing what is going on with them: looking, listening, touching, tasting or smelling them. We can get significantly different information and impressions from each of our senses, so we are well advised to become proficient in using all of them. Let's go through them in turn.

Watch what they look like, how healthy they look, how calm or upset, how energetic or tired, how animated or depressed, and how they interact with others. Look at the state that their rooms are in, how clean their clothes are, how tidy their school work is, and how personally clean they are.

> Use all five senses to notice your children. Get them to do the same as they pay attention to you.

Many clues come to us through really watching out children, many delights, too. Watching life is exquisite and children are so full of life.

We need to listen attentively to our children. What are they saying? What do they *mean* by what they are saying? Are they saying something important or trivial? Notice if they are telling us more by what they are *not* saying than what they *are* saying. How are they saying what they are saying? Words alone don't carry the full message. Do they sound calm, anxious, depressed, excited, loving, scared, sad, happy, hopeful, uncertain, or angry? Also, listen to what they say to friends and family. Listen to how they sound through the walls! You will hear them. Listen for changes in this.

Touch them and allow them to touch you. How do they feel to you? What do you feel about them as you touch them? Do they feel confident with touch? Do they respond well to being touched by you? Do they feel secure, needy, distant, repulsing, attractive, available, open, or closed to you as you touch each other. Many clues come through a hand on an arm, or leaning against someone for a moment, or through a quick hug. Notice their styles of moving around. Do they bump into things, are they sure-footed, graceful and coordinated?

Also, notice the taste and smell of them. Some people find this an unusual suggestion, while others know they rely on this as a primary measure of what is going on with their children. It is probably their smells that we will notice most easily of the two, although taste and smell seem to trigger each other. Their aromas are very present and relate to much more than hygiene. Most children and adults have consistent aromas, any changes to which can act as useful signals. Marked changes in aroma often indicate important emotional changes. So, be alert: do they smell sweet, sour, bitter, salty, foul or poisonous? Noticing how their rooms smell is another good indication of what is going on with them.

## Messages for children

'Wash/shower/bathe every day.'
'Keep your room clean, neat and tidy.'
'Make sure your clothes are fresh and clean at all times.'
'Change your socks and underwear every day.'

## A welcoming home

Everyone contributes to the atmosphere. We can make sure that it is full of beautiful things to look at, appealing sounds, enjoyable textures, delicious things to taste and enticing smells. Each family member can do at least one thing a day to beautify the home.

# Active listening

To make strong links with our children as we talk, it is best to use all five senses. We mean this literally. We need to keep looking at them, listening to them, touching them from time to time and, for some, staying aware of their taste/smell. Expecting and encouraging them to do the same is also important. These exchanges through our senses are what keep us linked to each other. Here are some things you can say to do this.

- While looking at them, we say, 'Look at me as you're talking to me', or 'Look at me while I'm talking to you'.
- As we listen attentively, we say, 'I'm listening to what you're saying. Listen to me, too'.
- During our talks, we reach out and touch them occasionally; we encourage them to do the same with us.

The mothers or fathers who pay full attention will know much more about their children than those who don't. Think of the fathers and mothers who always have their attention elsewhere when their children talk to them. For example, they watch the TV, listen to the radio, keep cooking, or read a newspaper at the same time. Parents who pay full attention to their children, will stop doing distracting things, face their children and truly engage. Naturally, it works both ways and we are usually best to insist on similar attentiveness from our children to us.

## How to listen actively

Two simple approaches help us ensure we are actively paying attention.

**We pay attention to what is said, and we respond to it.** That is, we stay on the same subject as our children. We do not change the subject.

- 'I'm feeling angry, Dad', says the son. 'Oh, you'll be all right. Pass the wrench, son.' This is a complete change of subject and is not effective listening.

- 'I'm feeling angry, Dad', says the son. 'Oh are you? Pass me the wrench, son, and tell me about it.' This is the same subject, but the listening is diluted by the task. Sometimes this is very helpful when a shared activity makes the talking easier. (An alternative is, 'Oh are you? What about waiting five minutes until I'm finished here, then I can give you my full attention'.)
- 'I'm feeling angry, Dad', says the son. 'Oh are you? I often used to feel angry when I was your age.' (There follows a long story about the father's youth.) This is not helpful as it shifts the focus away from the boy and completely onto the father.

*We also pay attention to the way things are said.*

- 'I'm feeling sad, Dad', says the son. 'Yes you're sounding sad to me. Tell me some more.' This is attentive and relating to the feelings generally.
- 'I'm feeling sad, Dad', says the son. 'You're feeling sad.' This often encourages the child to say more about the sadness specifically.
- 'I'm feeling sad, Dad', says the son. 'You sound sad to me and you also sound a bit angry.' The statement can get the son to explore what else is going on and to express more about either feeling.

# How to encourage expressiveness in our children

Four simple guidelines can help us encourage our children to express themselves. Each of them involves paying slightly different attention to what they are saying and how they are saying it.

*1. When you want a thoughtful response ask a question.*

- 'What do you think about that?
- 'What are you feeling?'
- 'What did you do next?'
- 'How much did that cost?'

*2. When you want to go with the flow and encourage self-expression, make statements.*

- 'Say more.'
- 'Go on.'
- 'You look upset and sound it too.'
- 'You're telling me that you ...'

*3. When you want to encourage expressiveness without influencing the content of what they say, repeat all or some of what they have just said.*

- 'You think you will go now.'
- 'You don't like what he said to you.'
- 'You felt very angry and then started to think about getting even.'
- 'You felt excited and want to go out and play.'

*4. Stay silent to show respect and to become strongly present with people.*

- Keep looking at the person, making your look attentive and receptive.
- Possibly nod your head a little.
- Stay relaxed and wait for the next move to occur naturally, in either of you.
- Say with your posture, 'I am here and with you'.

# Two examples of paying attention actively

Let's put this together in a couple of examples.

## Graham and the pups

In bounces Graham, all smiles and obviously very excited.

'Mum!'

'Hi! Well you look excited about something!' She makes her statements to encourage a flow-on effect from his high spirits and to get him talking.

'You know that bitch up the street. Well, she's had her pups and Mrs Grant says I can have one.' He stops and looks expectantly, but a cloud appears in his eyes as he seems to remember conversations about puppy care and who will have to do it all.

Mother chooses to go with the excitement for a while though. She is enjoying sharing the pleasure with Graham. 'So you really want one of these puppies.'

'Oh yes. They're so beautiful. You should see them and feel how soft they are. It won't be any trouble and I'll do everything, I promise.' He uses his eyes, sparkling with excitement and hope, to good effect.

'You really want one of these puppies.' Mother is still wanting to go with the flow and to tap off some of this lovely energy. She and Graham's father have already decided that now is the time. But before talking about their terms and conditions, she wants Graham to be a little less highly charged.

'I really, really, really want one. You should see the one I want. He already knows me. He was crawling all over me and he came when I called him.'

Mother stays attentively silent, open to her son and sharing his excitement with him. Then she says, 'Tell me what else he did'.

Graham talks excitedly with little encouragement for three minutes more.

When he seems to have discharged some of his energy, his mother says, 'So have you thought about where he could go?' She asks the question to get him thinking about things. This would have the effect of toning him down a little more, so she can move the discussion onto practicalities.

'Well, I thought he could sleep in the laundry to begin with. Then, when he's old enough, we could get a kennel and he can sleep out in the yard. I'll do everything, Mum. I promise I will. You won't have to do a thing.'

This mother doesn't fall for that, but she knows Graham will do his share. 'And who's going to bath him, and get up in the middle of the night for the first few months to take him into the yard for a pee?'

'Oh, I'll do that,' he said before she'd finished, although he had spoken before 'getting up in the middle of the night' was mentioned. This changed his expression considerably.

Mother draws him out on this a little. 'You don't look very enthusiastic about getting up.'

'Well, I don't know if I'll wake up, and you know if I don't get enough sleep, then I fall asleep all the next day.' He was looking sheepish and a little pleadingly at his mother.

In fact, he was right and he was only seven, so she said, 'I'm sure your father and I can work something out with you so we all share things. Now what about training? You will both have to go to obedience school.' She rather enjoyed the thought of Graham going to obedience school.

From his response, so, apparently, did he.

Eight weeks later the puppy arrived.

## Eliza's night off

Eliza, a fifteen-year-old, is making hard work of her homework. She wants to watch TV, but has to finish an essay. After a few exchanges with her father, she very reluctantly goes off to her room to do it. Appearing ten minutes later, she is obviously angry and sulky.

'It's just not fair. I've always got too much homework. Why can't I have a night off?'

Father thinks that any of these three statements might be fertile ground for close questioning. He realises, however, that trying to have a factual, practical discussion at this point is futile. Also, because she is so angry, sending her back to her room to get on with the job is unlikely to work. So he decides to draw her out, to tap off some of the energy. 'You don't think it's fair.'

'No I don't. Mrs Bryson does this deliberately. She gives us something every night.' Eliza sounds sour and petulant. 'She doesn't care how much we work in class. She always gives us more to do at home.'

Father gets the idea and puts it into words, 'She just likes to make your life miserable.' He pauses, noting his daughter's nodding head and thinking she is now calm enough to start to see sense. 'I guess that she spent weeks planning how to interfere with you watching this TV program tonight.' Warming lovingly to this theme, he says, 'In fact I think I'd better check with your mother just to make sure that she did ring us to be certain she had the right night.'

Eliza began to look puzzled when her father was part of the way through this and by the end was smiling and giggling a bit. 'Oh Dad, you know I don't mean that. You're just being silly.'

'Then tell me what it is that is really going on.' This is like a question, but is put in a way that will keep her flow going. He wondered about asking, 'Okay, so what is really going on?' but decided this would block her from the lightness that the fun had stimulated.

'I do want to watch the TV, but really the trouble is that I don't have any ideas about the assignment. It's just a stupid assignment.'

'You're saying the assignment is stupid because you can't do it,' Father says, arching an eyebrow. 'Could it be the other way around and that's what is provoking you?'

'Yes, I guess you're right,' she concedes with a little good grace. 'The trouble is I don't know where to start.'

'Is there some way I can help. Maybe if you go and get the book and show me what it's about, I can help you get started. Do you want to do that?'

'Yes, Dad. Thanks.' And off she goes. By this time, she is considerably calmer and probably ready to do her essay.

## Messages for children

'Stay alert. Notice what's going on around you.'

'Be responsive to others.'

'Reply when spoken to.'

'Take others into account in what you do.'

### Entertaining themselves

Your children come in and say with a whinge in their voices, 'Mum/Dad, I'm bored', or 'I haven't got anything to do'. The invitation is to get us to come up with things to entertain them. It is our job after all!

Reply, **'So what could you do to have fun?'**

Then you can discuss their ideas. For example, you can respond to, **'There's nothing to do'** by surprising them with, **'Well that's great. Sit and do nothing. It's wonderful to sit and explore what's going on inside us'.**

This is true of course, but you might get howls of outrage.

You could also suggest, **'What about going into your room, (or wherever the toys and other entertainments are kept) and look at all the things you haven't got to do. Then come back and tell me what isn't there'.**

This usually gets a laugh, however, it is best only done with children older than seven, who are developing an ironic sense of humour.

# Chapter 7

# Repeating ourselves

Repeating ourselves is a very simple and important part of parenting, yet it causes more upsets than many other issues.

- 'They accuse me of nagging and I know they're right.'
- 'When I was a kid, I didn't like my mum and dad doing it, so I don't want to myself.'
- 'Why can't they just do what they are supposed to without me having to remind them?'

Read on if you want 'good reasons' to nag, harp and make a fuss.

# Learning relies on repetition

Take particular notice of the next two sentences. *Children learn through repetition. They cannot learn well without it.* This is the reason that they get us to repeat things many times. This is also the justification for nagging, if you need one.

Just notice what babies do. They repeat everything hundreds and thousands of times. The hand goes into the mouth and out again – over and over. The toy is shaken, the toes are examined, the head is turned. Everything is repeated. Doing these things repeatedly actually lays down and strengthens neural pathways in the body. Good coordination and effective body control rely on these pathways and, therefore, on these activities. Without the repetitive physical activity, the pathways do not develop as needed.

Because our children have to repeat things so they can learn, we have to repeat things, too, so they can learn from us.

Our experience is that all learning follows a similar pattern. It all relies on repetition. Some important areas in which repetition is crucial to help children learn are:

- patterns of behaviour
- physical skills
- how to relate to others
- remembering certain types of things
- talking, reading, writing, drawing, doing arithmetic
- relating in different ways with different people
- household duties
- making decisions
- following through on commitments
- school work
- ways of thinking about things
- ways of expressing themselves.

The more often children do something, the more strongly they are learning to do it. Our parental job includes doing our best to get them to repeat what is important for them to learn. Our guidance, encouragement and corrections all contribute to them learning well.

- When they spontaneously do something we want them to do, we encourage them so as to get them to do it, again and again and again. (For example, they are friendly and welcoming with visitors.)
- When they spontaneously do something that we don't want them to do, we discourage them from doing it, and encourage them to do what we want instead, again and again and again. (For example, they ignore visitors and go off to their rooms. So we encourage them to stay and say, 'Hello', to entertain other children of their ages, and only to go off to their rooms if released to do so.)
- When they spontaneously don't do something that we want them to do, we keep encouraging them to do it. (For example, they don't spontaneously go in and say 'Hello' and shake hands with visitors the way we want them to. So we teach them how to do it and then remind them to do it with everyone who visits.)

(See Chapter 1, 'Parenting with love', Chapter 2, 'The discipline sequence', and Chapter 3, 'Standing to decide' for guidance on how to do this.)

## Things to repeat

It is both normal and important for us repeatedly to show them how to do up buttons, tell them what to say and how to say it, get them to look where they are going, remind them to do their household jobs and a myriad of other things.

Repeating ourselves is not a sign that we are inadequate, nor that our children have nothing active between the ears.

It is also normal and important to repeat all the messages we want them to use for inner guidance. Here is a sample:

- Be on time.
- Put it back where you got it from.
- Go and have fun.
- Have you fed the dog (cat, bird)?
- Go and do your homework.
- Talk in a normal voice
- Remember to give me your school notices.
- Speak clearly.
- Have you washed your hands?
- Look for how you can make the situation better.
- Avoid making situations worse.
- If you're unkind to people, they probably won't want to play with you.
- Do what I tell you immediately.
- Wait your turn.
- Drive carefully.
- Come home on time.
- Think before you act and work out the likely consequences.
- Share and cooperate.
- Think of other people too.

As a timely reminder, we know that most children do learn easily and well in some areas. All learn more easily in some areas than others. We recommend that you notice where they do learn easily, or more easily – and celebrate.

## It does work eventually

At 23, Petra used some greasy tools belonging to her boyfriend. She tried unsuccessfully to wash her hands under the tap. As a last resort she picked up some soap which worked immediately. Her mother's voice said, 'Always use soap', and she finally realised that her mother was right.

# Take heart

Persistence is well worthwhile, even in the midst of repetitious exchanges, when we get the impression that the process will go on forever. These impressions may explain why so many parents find this part of the job so challenging. However, as we persist, our children are affected.

- **When we are repeating, they are learning.** After a few years (let's say, 30!) you will be able to notice progress. Just remember what you were repeating a few years ago. You are likely to notice that you are only repeating some of this now. The rest is no longer necessary, because they are doing routinely what they are supposed to do.

- Also, when they repeat, so that we will repeat, it is as if **they are asking for more of their favourite desserts**. Don't let the fuss they make fool you. It might be an odd way of saying, 'More please'. But this is what they are saying. And the intensity of what they do, shows us the intensity of their desire for their 'just desserts'.

- **As we persist, they also learn to persist in their own lives.** The learning comes directly from us. Many a child has benefited from this. Unfortunately, also, many children have lacked follow-through as adults, because their parents gave up before they had learnt what they needed to learn.

## A handy answer

When our children tell us to 'Stop nagging', knowing what you now know, you have a wonderful answer. Give it with confidence and flair, pausing for effect between each point.

'Yes I am nagging. It's my job to nag. And I will keep on nagging until you do what I'm telling you to do. So do it now.'

You may still get to the point of thinking, as our parents often did, 'If I've told you once, I've told you a thousand times, ...' However, this is a good sign if you do. Congratulate, rather than berate yourself. At a thousand times, you are probably getting closer to the required number. If not, another thousand or so should just about do it!

# Eventually it's up to them

In the end, our children need to take over responsibility for reminding themselves and keeping themselves in line. Unless we are looking for lifelong jobs at their sides, we need to disengage eventually.

Many children make the transition naturally. This makes it easy for them and us. However, some children need a nudge to get them using what they have already got from us without our reminding them. And note that at times we may need to act strongly and decisively to achieve the desired results.

# Chapter 8

# Developing self-esteem

Most of us want our children to have good self-esteem. We want them to honour and value themselves realistically. Good self-esteem can form the foundation of many wonderful qualities, both during childhood and later in life.

This chapter contains a brief description of some things we can do to help our children develop self-esteem. We also discuss things to do to help deal with low self-esteem.

# How to build self-esteem

A variety of things contributes to our children developing self-esteem. Each of them makes a significant contribution, so it is a good idea to do some or all of them.

> Loving our babies with complete acceptance encourages the primary self-esteem of self-love.

## Give complete acceptance

The foundations of good self-esteem are laid from the beginning of life. Babies who are loved with complete, loving acceptance are well on the way to developing it. Children loved like this are able to withstand all sorts of trials and tribulations. The love we bathe them in saturates the bedrock of their personalities. (See Chapter 1, 'Parenting with love' for more on this.)

We love everything about our babies when we love with complete acceptance. We don't need reasons. We just do. We love our children just because they are there, and for who they are. What they do, does not influence this love. We will love them forever in this way, regardless of what they do. This does not mean that we like everything about them, however. Nevertheless, our responses to what they do only begins to become conditional at about eighteen months of age. (See Chapter 2, 'The discipline sequence'.)

## Provide active guidance and conditional acceptance

The next aspect of self-esteem comes from guiding our children to behave well with others. When they act according to the 'rules of living', we praise them. When they don't, we do things to discourage them from acting in those ways again. (See Chapter 2, 'The discipline sequence', Chapter 3, 'Standing to decide', and Chapter 4, 'Knowing when and how to act'.) In other words, we are selective about our responses.

In the process of becoming selective, however, we make sure of one very important distinction. We become selective about

**what they do**, while we continue to accept fully **who they are**.
Various themes are repeated with conditional acceptance.

- 'I love you and I don't like you behaving like this.'
- 'I like you doing that.'
- 'Well done', or 'You have done well.'
- 'Stop doing that. I don't like you doing that. Do such and such.'

Children who are well guided, who get clear messages about what is acceptable and what is not, usually feel confident with others. They feel secure in this, because they know where they stand with people. They know how to behave and how not to behave. They know what others like and dislike.

- Roy was a well-loved child, who nevertheless was very unsure of himself with children the same age. He used to go out of his way to avoid contact with them by playing alone in the schoolyard and staying on the edges of things in the classroom. Whatever he did at home was accepted, but at school he found most of what he did created trouble. As soon as his parents and teachers started an active program of teaching him how to relate to the other children, he became much more confident and more accomplished socially.
- Thea was also loved at home and as unsure of herself as Roy. The way she dealt with this was through boldness. She pretended everything was all right and used to boss the other children around, bullying any of them who did not do what she wanted them to do. When her parents became systematic in challenging her bullying and tantrum-throwing behaviour at home, she became much more settled on the inside. Her confidence rose, because she was getting the guidance she needed about what to do and what not to do with others.

> Active guidance and conditional acceptance of our children's behaviour encourages the self-esteem that comes from relating well to others.

## Expect self-control

People have self-control when they can make decisions and can follow through on them. Their decisions lead to the necessary actions. The sense of mastery this produces results in great self-esteem. It is the self-esteem of knowing that they can rely on themselves to perform well.

Think of the children you currently know who do what they do very easily. They don't seem to have any difficulties. They seem able to do whatever they set out to do. Compare these children to those who don't have the necessary abilities, who struggle to perform. Usually the differences in self-esteem between these two groups are very marked.

All of this comes naturally to some children. However, most need to learn it. They learn it directly from us, through our setting standards and limits, and our following through to ensure that our children act accordingly. By contrast, children with ineffective parents are much less likely to develop personal mastery and the self-esteem that goes with it. (See Chapter 2, 'The discipline sequence', for more on this.)

Loving discipline encourages the self-esteem that comes from making decisions and following through on them.

## Promote confidence in ability

Mastering skills can produce great confidence in children. Much self-esteem can arise from acting skilfully. We can support our children's abilities by applauding each new achievement and also by providing opportunities to challenge and extend them. Putting lots of effort into this usually pays off.

Nevertheless, we are wise to maintain a balance in this. If we push them to learn things that are beyond their current abilities, we can undermine their confidence. At the same time, if we hold them back, they will not have the opportunity to learn to meet and overcome new challenges.

- Even when only in primary school, Renata was expected to study maths every weekend under her father's guidance. In itself, this might have worked out well. Unfortunately, her father had no idea of what young children can learn. He set work that was far beyond her capacities. He compounded the problems for her by criticising and punishing her for not performing well. By the time she was an adult, her confidence in her ability to do things was seriously damaged.

- Oscar took ages to learn how to tie his shoelaces. His parents decided that while velcro would be easier, it was an important skill for him to learn, so they persisted. They got him to do as much as he could each time, and then one of them would finish the rest for him. Eventually, when they decided that it was time for him to do it all on his own, he resisted. 'I can't do it, Mum,' he said tearfully. But they persisted. His joy and sense of achievement when he succeeded was a great reward for all of them.

> Teaching children skills promotes the self-esteem that comes from personal mastery.

## Insist on a contribution

Something happens inside us all when we can contribute to the people and systems that support us. Our contributions set up a circuit in which a flow develops in both directions, rather than just one. Many people are aware of the dissatisfaction that mounts when they give perpetually to others; many people are also aware of a dissatisfaction that mounts when they take too much from others.

The mutuality of sharing and exchanging of service has a wonderful effect on children. Instead of being dependent and having to rely on others, they can develop a sense of making worthwhile contributions to their families. As they get older, they can expand this to making valuable contributions to their schools, local neighbourhoods, their countries and then to the world.

The way we help children initially develop the self-esteem that comes from giving valued service to others, is through getting them to do chores at home. We have already mentioned in several places, the importance of using chores as a way of preparing children for living in the world as adults. The contribution to self-esteem that our children experience is another good reason for doing this. Those who don't know this from experience miss a great deal.

> *Maria had not been used to contributing. Her parents used to think that, 'Children are only young once, so we'll leave her to herself to enjoy it while she can'. After speaking to us, they decided to change what they had been doing, for Maria's benefit. They all sat down together and, much to her dismay, worked out a set of jobs for her to do. She was angry for a week or so and not very pleasant. After several weeks, they were all much happier. The sharing was mutually enjoyable and satisfying. Maria said to her mother at the sink one day, 'I didn't realised how much you and Dad did. I feel quite upset that I used to go and listen to music in my room or watch TV. And I enjoy doing all this now, too.'*

Doing chores helps our children develop the self-esteem that comes from making a valued contribution to others.

## Encourage belonging

A sense of belonging is fundamentally important in self-esteem. Most children with good self-esteem have this. Many with low self-esteem do not. Belonging is experienced as 'I am important to (name)'.

What gives children this sense of belonging? The first element is having someone who is actively involved with them, who cares about them. The second is that this someone is accessible. The children can get to their special people to talk or do whatever else they need to do.

Interestingly, the belonging comes as much from the struggles children have with caring people, as it does from the good times. This makes sense, however, if you think about it. When we care enough to struggle with our children, to get them to do things that they may not want to do, we are very obviously saying, 'You belong with us and so you will do such and such'. Parents who avoid the tougher things like this do not convey this kind of belonging with the same strength.

Parents who are accessible and care enough to do both the tough and the soft things help their children develop the self-esteem that comes from belonging with someone.

## Support realistic self-assessment

To have good self-esteem, children need a realistic impression of themselves. They need a grounded evaluation of their qualities and talents, and their attitudes and values in relation to others. With a realistic understanding of themselves, they are likely to be sensitive and aware of others, and to have a humble view of themselves. This is different from the arrogance, conceit, self-importance, selfishness and insensitivity that children can develop if their self-esteem becomes distorted.

The dependability of self-esteem is promoted by teaching our children to assess themselves and their talents realistically.

They are encouraged to be realistic by us being realistic with them. We need to give them practical, realistic and honest assessments of how they are acting, of the skills and talents they have, and of the effects on others of the things that they do. It is most important that we do this.

- 'No. You didn't do that well. You need to pay more attention here.'
- 'I realise that you feel you are right. But you are not. I will tell you what is true.'
- 'You did that wonderfully well.'
- 'Liking yourself is great. But condemning others is very unpleasant for them and they will react to you doing that.'
- 'There are some things that you cannot do yet. This is one of them. It is important that you not pretend that you can do things that you can't do.'

## Summary

We help to make sure that children have good self-esteem by:
- loving them with complete acceptance
- giving them loving guidance on how to relate to others
- setting standards and limits to promote self-control
- teaching them the skills they need
- giving them real jobs to do at home
- spending lots of time with them and including them in our lives
- providing realistic assessments of their actual abilities.

### The other side

Self-esteem is not a cure-all for problems, nor is its absence the cause of all problems. To solve some problems, children may need to develop other qualities, too. Sometimes having 'good self-esteem' even creates problems when children start to overrate their abilities.

# Low self-esteem

What can we do to help turn things around with children who see themselves in a bad light? We have five general suggestions.

## Acceptance

Use complete, loving acceptance at all appropriate times. While they may not
accept us doing this openly at the time, it does make a difference. The idea is to persist through the days, weeks, months and, for some children, years that it takes.

- Say things like, 'I love you', 'You are a beautiful person', 'I like being with you'.
- Give them plenty of hugs and physical affection.
- Talk from the heart.
- Look lovingly at them.

## Praise

Give true praise by acknowledging talents. Avoid exaggeration and false reassurance.

- 'You are sensitive, intelligent, capable, sporty.'
- 'You look great, dress well, do creative things.'
- 'You are dedicated, flexible, reliable, quick-witted.'

## Guidance

Program the things that you want to become true. The idea of this is to think of things they are already doing and tell them that they do them. This will help build strength from strength. Avoid doing this to soothe or pretend. Also, give true examples of what you say.

- 'You remember well.'
- 'You like people and get along well with them.'
- 'You understand things easily.'
- 'You persist in the face of challenges.'

# Sensitivity and realism

Deal with dejection and self-doubt directly by using sensitivity and realism.

- *Encourage the expression of feelings.* Do this by concentrating on the feelings for a while, not moving directly to problem-solving. (See Chapter 6, 'Paying active attention'.)

- *Give realistic feedback.* Our children know the truth. They know when we are making things up, or just saying something so they will feel better. Two examples are, 'You are capable and likeable', or 'No, you don't have many friends yet, that's true'. You might also add other thoughts, when they are ready for them, such as, 'Well you do act provocatively', or 'If you don't go and play with her, she won't know that you like her'.

- *Make practical suggestions about how to deal with things.* The more concrete and helpful these are the better. For example, 'If you want to make friends with her, say "Hello" every day when you see her. And smile and act in a friendly way'.

- *Follow up.* We do this to check that they are trying the suggestions we have made. As we follow up, three simple steps help:

  1. Talk to them to find out how they got on. Don't assume you know.
  2. Pinpoint and celebrate successes, even minor ones. Separate what they actually did from what they feel they did.
  3. Identify difficulties and deal with them as above.

# Chapter 9

# Managing siblings

Having more than one child can add great richness to everyone in a family. All sorts of pleasures and opportunities automatically arise that are not there with an 'only child'. Children learn through the repeated, intense exposure to each other that living together produces. This is extremely important in later life.

In this chapter, we mainly concentrate on how to deal with rivalries, competition, jealousies and other challenges usually known as 'sibling rivalry'.

# Basic positions

Resolution between children is promoted by understanding three basic positions. These positions apply equally to adults.

## Each of our children is different

Complete satisfaction in their lives, or resolution of any difficulties between them, relies on each of them understanding what we do from their own points of view. Whenever we get involved in situations with our children, it is most important that we find out what is going on for each of them. Their versions of events, motivations, understandings, feelings and goals might all be different. We need to check these, if we are to make what we do relevant to each of them.

- For the fourteen-year-old, keeping the seven-year-old out of his room might be what he wants, while the seven-year-old wants some time to play with his older brother.
- 'I didn't mean to knock over his Lego tower,' says the five-year-old, 'I was in a hurry to get past.' The two-and-a-half-year-old just keeps crying, clearly experiencing the event as an added insult during a day of working very hard at suffering. She is clearly beyond reasons making a difference at this point.
- 'She did it,' shouts one child. 'What a lie,' says the other, 'he did.' We wonder who did and, if we can, it's our job to find out who. Maybe both did, or someone else entirely.

## 'Where to from here?'

Whenever more than one child is involved, they always have a collective issue to sort out. They need to work out 'where to from here?'. How they will relate to each other from then onwards so they get along well is always important. We get the children to consider how both to promote ease and to manage likely conflicts in the future. A great way to do this is to get them to make agreements with each other. (See Chapter 2, 'The discipline sequence' and Chapter 3, 'Standing to decide' for more on this.) Whatever agreements they each make, need to deal with the issues from the points of view of each child making them. The agreements will help to guide future exchanges.

- One says, 'I'll knock before I come into your room in future. I won't just barge in'. The other says, 'I won't just yell at you to go away, if I don't want you to come in. I'll tell you "I'm busy" and give you a time when I'll be free'.
- One agrees, 'I'll talk politely to you from now on. Even when I'm angry, I won't call you names'. The other says, 'Good. I feel upset when you yell. But I'll talk to you first, even if you're angry. I won't just run to Mummy or Daddy.'

## Sibling rivalry is normal

Children learn many important lessons as they learn to handle each other. That they squabble, compete and struggle with each other is not a sign that anything is wrong. Any two children are likely to do this at times. The important thing for us to do as parents is to teach them how to move through these kinds of situations to resolution. When all children involved have made clear what their points of view are and have made specific agreements with each other, then the process is finished.

### Things siblings can learn
To play together and entertain each other
To share and cooperate
To cope with missing out and with difference
To love and support each other
To solve problems with each other
To learn through copying, competing, and teaching

# Sorting things out

When encouraging changed behaviour between children, or when sorting out problems between them, we follow four basic steps. Sometimes the order of the steps is different from the one here; however, each step has a unique contribution to make.

1. Stop the action.
2. Get each child's story.
3. Parent each child.
4. Get them to talk to each other, to apologise and to make agreements.

## Stop the action

This is most important, particularly if disagreements, or serious squabbles or fights are involved. Many parents have been told or have decided that it is best to leave children to work things out for themselves. Until all the children involved are experienced in sorting out their problems with each other, however, our experience is that this is not a good idea. Once they are experienced, on the other hand, we find that a time comes when we leave them to it. Possible things to do:

- Say, 'Stop what you're doing and come over here'.
- Move over to them and tell them to stop.
- Move over to them, get between them, if necessary, and insist they stop and pay attention to you.

## Get each child's story

Asking each child his or her point of view is important. Useful questions include:

- What have you been doing?
- What do you think is going on?
- How did you both start? Then what did you (he/she) do? Then what?
- What did you do? Why did you do it?
- What do you want to happen now?
- What do you want (name) to do from now on?

*A **word** to **the** wise:* Our experience is that there are no innocent Victims, so we parents are well advised to avoid taking sides. Our experience is that the apparent Victim always does something to provoke what occurs. A story illustrates this well.

> *A small boy called Colin came home from school one day, still outraged that a fellow student had punched him in the stomach. He was looking for sympathy from his father. Colin was surprised when his father's response was not sympathy, but a question: 'What did you do to get punched in the stomach?' After very little talk, Colin revealed that he had elbowed the other boy in the ribs just before getting punched. This somewhat changed the impression Colin was trying to create!*

## Parent each child

Once we know what each child intended to do and actually did, we can give guidance, suggest other ways of handling things, make simple rules on what to do from now on, and set incentives and consequences if these will help. We may do quite a lot of this while getting the information, too. When, for example, they try to interrupt each other, we can say things like, 'No you wait your turn. I will talk to you next', or 'If you keep interrupting while we're talking, you'll go over there and "stand to decide" that you will wait patiently. You've already had your say'. This trains them in cooperative problem-solving.

For the best effect, the parenting and advice we give needs to be put so that each of the children understands it. The older the child, the more grown-up we can make our explanations and expectations.

Think about Colin again. The exchange may go like this. His father says, 'If you hurt people, you are very likely to get hurt yourself. So you keep your elbows to yourself from now on Colin.' Colin looks thoughtful. His father guesses what he might be thinking and adds, 'The other boy should not have hit you either. Neither of you should have done what you did'. Colin relaxes. Father continues, 'Now come over here so I can have a look at your tummy. While I do, you tell me what you will do from now on'. As his father checks for damage, he offers some appropriate sympathy. The instruction about future behaviour moves him to the next step of the process.

# Talk, apologies and agreements

## Talking to each other

Throughout the sorting-out process it is very helpful to get the children to talk directly to each other. Whenever they say something to us that they have not said to the other one(s), we can get them to say it directly. Also, when they have said it, but have not been listened to, we can get them to say it directly again and ensure that they are heard and responded to. It doesn't matter that they have witnessed the whole conversation with us. It still makes a difference for them to do it with each other. Two examples are:

- 'Tell Jim what you just told me. And Jim, as Shelly does, I want you to think about how you feel and tell her after she has finished.'
- 'What about saying that to Kath now. Kath, I want you to keep quiet as David tells you and listen carefully to what he is saying about how he felt. His feelings matter, too.'

## Apologies

Getting them to apologise to each other for any insensitivities, broken agreements, or for causing unwanted consequences is important. The act of apologising gets children to take responsibility for what they have done. It also helps to reveal any resistance in our children to them accepting their parts in the events. Examples are:

- 'I'm sorry for hitting you.'
- 'I apologise for standing in front of the TV so you couldn't see.'
- 'I didn't mean to stop you going to the movies. I didn't realise what I did would stop you and I'm sorry.'

## Agreements

Once they are clear with each other on what they were doing and have apologised, we get them to make agreements with each other about the future. These help to pull together all the discussions and lead to change from then on. It would be a pity to spend all this time 'for nothing'!

As we have already discussed in several places, keeping the concentration on what they want with each other is worthwhile. This applies in the agreements they make as much as with anything else. So get them to tell each other what they like about each other as part of making the agreement. It helps children break through the 'oh yuck' barrier that some of them build up about the expression of love and affection.

The conversation may go like this. 'I like playing with you and want to have fun. I'll share my toys with you from now on if they are in the family room. I'll keep all my toys that I don't want you to play with in my room,' says the first child. 'I like that, because I like playing with you, too. I'll enjoy sharing my toys with you. I'll keep my hands off your toys, when they are in your room,' says the second child.

## Take the time

As you have probably guessed, the process can be time-consuming. However, the benefits are well worth the time it takes. Think of two things: First, if you don't teach them how to do it, then they are likely to keep having difficulties that you will need to deal with. So you will end up having to get involved anyway. Deliberately following the four-steps process will teach them how to manage increasingly for themselves. Second, the children who have this kind of training grow up with highly developed capacities to act assertively on behalf of themselves, to remain sensitive to others, to negotiate for what they want and to handle themselves well when they are experiencing conflict with others. What a wonderful legacy from a few hours of structured talk when they are young.

# If their stories disagree ...

As we all know, this is very unlikely to occur! However, when it does, how can we best handle things. We suggest the following, again not necessarily in the order given.

- Get reports from independent witnesses if possible. If you witnessed what occurred, you don't need other witnesses.
- Decide if both stories are likely to be true. Also, remember that sometimes both are right.
- If they can't both be true, tell them that what they are saying is not possible, that one or both of them is distorting the truth. Find out if this leads to a change of story.
- If so, then carry on from there.
- If not, then consider what is usually true with the children involved. This does not make it correct, but it may lead to progress. You can say, 'Well Jenny, you have often done such and such in the past, why should I not think that you have done it again this time. I've only got what you and (name) are telling me, so how can I know?' Find out if her answer gives you any more clues.
- We can also make guesses and tell them what our guesses are. We do this to test their reactions. As we do, we parent them on what we think they should have done and should do in future. Even if we guess wrong, they get more good parenting.
- We could tell them to 'stand to decide' to make sure that what they are saying is complete and true. The trouble with this is that the 'innocent' suffer along with the 'guilty'. Under some circumstances this might still be justified, however.
- If they continue to disagree, then we need to stay alert in the future so we witness what they do and don't need to rely on their stories. In the meantime, we parent them and set consequences and expect agreements that relate to their respective stories. We point out to them that we have to do this because we do not know the truth from them.

The following story shows how the fullness of time tends to correct unrecognised patterns. It also shows that it is best to find what our children have actually done with each other.

*We were visiting friends. We were all having breakfast. The son, Maurice, kicked his older sister, Helena, under the table. He made sure that his parents could not see what he had done. Helena yelped with pain and accused Maurice loudly. He, all injured innocence, suffered tearfully for the benefit of his parents and denied his guilt. Both parents said almost in unison, 'Helena, stop making things up'. Helena was outraged, but was clearly used to not being believed, because she immediately slumped in dejected submission. We also spoke in duet to Maurice, just after his parents, saying, 'That's a lie. I saw you kick Helena'. Her face was a picture of relief and amazement that she was believed. His was of incredulous rancour that we did not go along with his lie. We had broken 'the social rule' that guests should stay quiet at times like this. Maurice was counting on our silence to add weight to his position. Our response, however, exposed his guilt in an ongoing persecution. Our friends were also surprised, particularly at how long they had accepted Maurice's version of events. Their eyes were open from then on.*

## Messages for children

'Always tell the whole truth.'

'Lying, or distorting what anyone did, only confuses and complicates matters.'

'Talk about your experience; you know what you thought, felt and did.'

'You are going to sort this out, so accept that and get on with it.'

# Other important guidelines

Here is a brief list of other guidelines that might help you in various situations.

- Set standards of behaviour between children and enforce them. For example, expect real sensitivity and respect between them. Also, remember to get real apologies and commitments to change, whenever they are necessary.

- Repeated patterns of difficulty between children frequently reflect conflicts within or between parents. We need to get our own acts together under these circumstances.

- Get the children to act kindly, lovingly, sensitively and with caring as a general way of living. With this as a background, many minor difficulties are much easier to deal with.

- Get them to do things regularly that involve sharing, even the older ones with the younger ones.

- Encourage individuality as well as cooperation.

- Help them learn to solve their problems together without your intervention.

- Tell them that it is all right for them to have different privileges. Underline that they are different people and different ages.

- Inequality is a fact of life. Deal with them according to their actual needs and the facts of situations, not only according to what they want or think they are missing. Practise acting in a matter-of-fact way about this. Your acceptance of this will help them accept it too.

Stay grounded in and open to reality. If they say, 'He's always allowed to do more than me', we say, 'Yes that's right. He's older than you. And that's okay. Your turn will come'.

- Use 'standing to decide' whenever you need to focus attention, encourage thinking, get acceptance, deal with entrenched resistance, shift children from nastiness, or stop the action. You can have all the children involved in an incident 'standing to decide' at the same time. We remember one time when we did not have any more space around the walls! About ten kids all got involved in something together and kept producing uproar until 'standing to decide' calmed them all down.

- When children feel jealous, get them to concentrate on what they want and on how to get it. Emphasise sharing. Jealous children often concentrate on what they are missing. They usually feel a mixture of anger, fear and sadness about what they are missing; and they feel blocked from feeling the love, or happiness they perceive someone else having with a third person. Getting them saying things like, 'Can I go next?' or 'Will you give me a cuddle too?' or 'I'd like to sit next to you, too. When can I?' often helps.

- Avoid trying to make things right for everyone. This can put us on a treadmill. All children need to learn to miss out at times and to accept this with good grace.

- Have a rule, 'Family membership carries with it the duty of giving proper respect to everyone. It is not a licence for abuse'. Some families' members behave very well with people outside the family, but not with the family members themselves.

When a child invokes the name of 'the Great God Fair' with the cry, 'It's not fair!', we reply simply and dispassionately, 'That's true. But it is just'. (We may need to explain what justice is, of course.)

# Acknowledgements

We have distilled the experience of many years into this book. Many hundreds of people have contributed to it and we thank everyone who has.

Jacqui Schiff was particularly significant in the early formation of some of Ken's approaches to parenting and we thank her for the part she played. Along with her, the people who have contributed most to the content are many hundreds of parents and children. We thank them for allowing us to observe them, for making themselves so wonderfully available to us and for their willingness to try our suggestions and find out if they worked.

Particular thanks go to Averil Coe, Sara Parsons, Steve and Shaaron Biddulph, and David Carman.

We thank all our colleagues and friends for their ongoing encouragement and support. We particularly thank Rex Finch of Finch Publishing for his initial idea to create the Busy Parents Series and for asking us to contribute the first two books from our work in *ParentCraft*. With his usual enthusiasm and professionalism he helped work out a plan to fit the necessary work into our already busy schedule.

A very grateful thank-you is also due to the many people who have given us feedback on *ParentCraft*, almost unanimously praising it and telling us both generally and specifically the assistance it has given them.

Finally, we thank everyone who contributed by reading the manuscript in its various stages of completion. We value all their feedback.

# Recommended reading

Amelia D. Auckett, *Baby Massage*, Hill of Content, Melbourne, 1981

Steve Biddulph, *Manhood: A Book About Setting Men Free*, Finch Publishing, Sydney, 1994

Steve Biddulph, *Raising Boys: Why Boys Are Different - and How to Help Them Become Happy and Well-balanced Men*, Finch Publishing, Sydney, 1997

Steve Biddulph, *The Secret of Happy Children: A New Guide for Parents*, Bay Books, Sydney, 1984

Steve and Shaaron Biddulph, *More Secrets of Happy Children*, Harper Collins, Sydney, 1994

Rollow Browne and Richard Fletcher (ed.s), *Boys in Schools: Addressing the Real Issues Behaviour, Values and Relationships*, Finch Publishing, Sydney, 1995

Wendy Darvill and Kelsey Powell, *The Puberty Book: A Guide for Children and Teenagers*, Hodder and Stoughton, London, 1995

Carl H. Delacato, *A New Start for the Child with Reading Problems: A Manual for Parents*, David McKay Company, Inc., New York, 1970

Dr. Nora Duffield, *Talking to Kids...With Feeling: A Book for Adults and Children*, Random House, Auckland, 1995

Thomas Gordon, *Discipline That Works: Promoting Self-discipline in Children*, Plume, New York, 1991

Thomas Gordon, *PET: Parent Effectiveness Training*, New American Library Trade, New York, 1990

Muriel James and Dorothy Jongeward, *Born to Win: Transactional Analysis with Gestalt Experiments*, Addison-Wesley, Reading, 1971

Sheila Kitzinger, *Pregnancy & Childbirth*, Michael Joseph Limited, London, 1980

Sheila Kitzinger, *The Crying Baby: Why Babies Cry, How Parents Feel, What You Can Do About It*, Viking, London, 1989

Jo Lamble and Sue Morris, *Motherhood: Making It Work For You*, Finch Publishing, Sydney, 1999

Andrew Matthews, *Being Happy: A Handbook to Greater Confidence and Security*, Media Masters, Singapore, 1988

Andrew Matthews, *Making Friends: A Guide to Getting Along With People*, Media Masters, Singapore, 1990

Maria Pallotta-Chiarolli (ed.), *Girls Talk: Young Women Speak Their Hearts and Minds*, Finch Publishing, Sydney, 1998

Joseph Chilton Pearce, *Magical Child: Rediscovering Nature's Plan of Our Children*, Paladin Books, London, 1979

Warwick Pudney and Judy Cottrell, *Beginning Fatherhood: A Guide for Expectant Fathers*, Finch Publishing, Sydney, Australia, 1998

Phyllis York, David York and Ted Wachtel, *Toughlove*, Bantam Books, New York, 1983

Phyllis York, David York and Ted Wachtel, *Toughlove Solutions: Runaways, Sex, Suicide, Drugs, Alcohol, Abuse, Disrupted Families, Community Indifference*, Bantam Books, New York, 1985

# Biame Network

Biame Network Inc. is an international, non-profit, educational organisation. It is an Incorporated Association with members in many countries. Founded in 1984 by Ken and Elizabeth Mellor, its primary purpose is to take a spiritually-based approach to helping people integrate personal awakening with their day-to-day activities. The approaches developed within the Network are down-to-earth, practical and easily used by people living everyday lives in the modern world. They have their origins in a variety of traditions, but owe allegiance to none.

The Network's varied activities and programs enable people to use it as a resource for many different purposes. The wide-ranging techniques are drawn from many parts of the world in both the East and the West. Services are offered in areas that include personal health and well-being, self-management, parenting, teacher education, relationship development, financial and business management, community development, personal growth and change, spiritual evolution and practices, and advanced spiritual awakening.

Items related to parenting and other areas are available through the Network's shop.

All enquiries are welcome:

Biame Network, P.O. Box 271, Seymour, Victoria 3661, Australia.
Tel. + 61 3 5799 1198, Freecall (in Australia) 1800 244 254
Fax. + 61 3 5799 1132.
Email: biamenet@eck.net.au
Web site: www.biamenetwork.net

# Index

# Other Finch titles

## ParentCraft

In this practical and commonsense guide (now in its second edition) Ken and Elizabeth Mellor provide important parenting skills and tested ways for parents to deal with a wide range of family situations. They include insights into the cycles and stages of childhood as well as how our family backgrounds contribute to what we do. They explore other themes that relate to managing families, catering for the needs of parents and children, setting standards and limits, love and discipline, and integrating important values into parenting.

*ParentCraft: A practical guide to raising children well* (2nd edition). Ken and Elizabeth Mellor (2001) ISBN 1876451 19X

### Praise for ParentCraft:

'I have been recommending *ParentCraft* in the parenting classes I teach and in my private practice ... Over a period of nine months, the feedback I have received has been tremendously enthusiastic. *ParentCraft* is one of those special books that, once read, moves people to share it with others.' *Eric, USA*

'I read your book and can only say I wish you had written it 17 years ago! Maybe then I wouldn't be wishing for a rewind button for my teenager! I've passed my copy along to a friend who has a six-month-old boy.' *Rita, Hawaii, USA*

'The book is terrific – really accessible, well set out and packed with useful guidelines to parenting. Well done!' *Martin and Sue, UK*

## Busy Parents Series

The first two books in the Busy Parents Series – which provides concise and practical parenting information – are *The Happy Family* and *Easy Parenting*.

*The Happy Family* is about how to make family life enjoyable. In this book, Ken and Elizabeth Mellor suggest that our families are little communities in which children learn how to live in the wider world. The authors provide simple, easy-to-use ways to manage our families well. Their practical advice on how to do this includes:

- understanding and changing your family patterns
- creating balance between family life and work
- learning from your childhood experience of families
- handling family conflicts
- working together as a parenting team.

*The Happy Family*. Ken and Elizabeth Mellor ISBN 1876451 122

Visit our website (www.finch.com.au) to see current information about new titles in this series.

### Side by Side

The authors provide strategies for individuals and couples to identify and overcome common relationship problems, to help them communicate better with their partners and consider issues such as their expectations, commitment and attitude to their partner's qualities.
*Side by Side: How to think differently about your relationship.*
Jo Lamble and Sue Morris (2000) ISBN 1876451 092

### Motherhood

At times, many mothers may feel that their lives are out of control. *Motherhood* is designed to help women deal with the pressures of family life and the expectations of being a mum of children of all ages.
*Motherhood: Making it work for you.* Jo Lamble & Sue Morris (1999) ISBN 1 876451 03 3

### Girls' Talk

This is the book that every teenage girl should read. Over 150 young women contribute their thoughts and stories on relationships, bodies, families, school life, sex and love, prejudice, feminism and independence. *Girls' Talk: Young women speak their hearts and minds.* Maria Pallotta-Chiarolli (1998) ISBN 1 876451 02 5

### Raising Boys

In his international bestseller, author Steve Biddulph examines the crucial ways that boys differ from girls. He looks at boys' development from birth to manhood and discusses the parenting and guidance boys need. *Raising Boys: Why boys are different – and how to help them become happy and well-balanced men.* Steve Biddulph (1997) ISBN 0 646 31418 1

### Boys in Schools

Fifteen classroom teachers, from primary and secondary schools, provide positive accounts of how they changed boys' behaviour to improve learning, relationships and the whole school environment. *Boys in Schools: Addressing the real issues – behaviour, values and relationships.* Rollo Browne & Richard Fletcher (eds) (1995) ISBN 0 646 23958 9

### Bullybusting

This practical book aims to help children develop understandings and skills which can be used throughout their lives. It contains special activity pages and is suitable for children of primary and secondary school age. *Bullybusting: How to help children deal with teasing and bullying.* Evelyn Field (1999) ISBN 1 876451 04 1

## Manhood

This bestselling book has had a profound effect on the lives of thousands of men and women around the world. Steve Biddulph discusses issues such as love and sexuality, being a father, finding meaning in work, making real friends and forming new partnerships with women. *Manhood: An action plan for changing men's lives.* (2nd edn) Steve Biddulph (1995) ISBN 0 646261 44 4

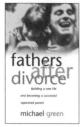

## Fathers After Divorce

This practical handbook includes straightforward checklists for separated fathers to use in overcoming problems and developing a positive outlook, as well as advice from many men on how to begin a new life.
*Fathers After Divorce: Building a new life and becoming a successful separated father.* Michael Green (1998) ISBN 1 876451 00 9

## Dealing with Anger

This book aims to help men solve their anger problems and eliminate the risk of anger-driven violence. A step-by-step program focuses on emotional healing, behaviour control and practical change. *Dealing with Anger: Self-help solutions for men.* Frank Donovan (1999) ISBN 1 876451 05 X

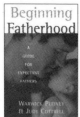

## Beginning Fatherhood

A warm and informative book for the man about to start the most important job of his life. It is full of practical and commonsense advice and encourages men to be active partners in the birth process. *Beginning Fatherhood: A guide for expectant fathers.* Warwick Pudney and Judy Cottrell. (1998) ISBN 1 876451 01 7

## On Their Own

For a young man, the absence of an involved father in his life can create a powerful sense of loss that he takes into adulthood. Such an absence (whether caused by his father's death, divorce, lack of time or interest) can lead to real difficulties in his adult relationships and his role as a parent. *On Their Own: Boys growing up underfathered.* Rex McCann (2000) ISBN 1876451 084

**FINCH**

Publishers of books on parenting, relationships and social issues

### Contact Finch Publishing

To see our latest titles or contact our authors, visit our website: www.finch.com.au. Finch titles are available in bookshops throughout Australia, New Zealand, South Africa and many countries in Asia. Alternatively write to us at P O Box 120, Lane Cove 1595, Australia. Phone (02) 9418 6247   Fax (02) 9418 8878.